Specific Action Steps & Strategies for Success From an Immigrant
Who is Living the American Dream

EFFICIENCY AND ORGANIZATION

TO ACHIEVE MORE IN LIFE

RUZANNA KRDILYAN HERNANDEZ, ED.D.

Higher Ground Books & Media
Springfield, Ohio.
http://highergroundbooksandmedia.com

Printed in the United States of America 2021

Specific Action Steps & Strategies for Success From an Immigrant
Who is Living the American Dream

EFFICIENCY AND ORGANIZATION
TO ACHIEVE MORE IN LIFE

RUZANNA KRDILYAN HERNANDEZ, ED.D.

Table of Contents

Introduction

When I was a teenager in the mid to late 1990s in middle school and high school, I wanted to be the best student I could be. I studied hard for my exams. I read and did the extra assignments that my teachers recommended. I tried going above and beyond on projects that were due. I did not have the resources as readily available to me as others.

There were significant financial barriers to overcome. As an immigrant child, I had to learn English while pursuing my studies. Besides language, it was challenging to learn and adapt to a new way of life in a new country. Most people I knew grew up like me; they did not have the resources readily available to them but still managed to make it through and find success. My parents did everything they could to help my sibling and me succeed in life. I will never forget how in the mid-1990s when computers were still not commonplace, my parents paid over $4,000 to purchase me a computer system from Sears. They understood how much a computer would help me in my educational endeavors and how hard I worked to succeed in getting good grades to go to college.

I carried my gritty attitude from middle school to high school to college. From 1998 to 2003, I earned my bachelor's degree while working full-time in the financial/insurance sector. It took me five years to earn a bachelor's degree, but I had to work full-time to support myself and my family – there was no way to decrease hours at work to give more time to school.

In the early 2000s, I got married, started a family, and decided to pursue a master's degree along with teaching credentials. I worked full-time while attending classes at the University of La Verne in Southern California. I juggled being a mom, a wife, a homeowner, a full-time employee at a school district while going to school. Time management was a huge factor. I understood the better I manage it, the more I would succeed. I earned my credentials to teach high school math and a master's degree.

The grittiness did not wear off. Midway into my teaching career, I realized I wanted to play a more significant role in the education system. I went back to the University of La Verne, this time, to pursue a doctoral degree in education and organizational leadership. Between 2013 and 2017, this was what I juggled all at the same time:

- Full-time teacher
- Mother
- Wife
- Small business owner
- 2nd master's degree
- Administrative credentials
- Doctoral degree
- Teaching 2 to 3 days per week at the adult school (evening classes for students pursuing their high school equivalency certificates)
- Parent Involvement Coordinator at the high school where I worked
- Testing Coordinator
- Department Chair of Mathematics
- Instructional Leadership Team Coordinator
- Recognition programs coordinator

In July of 2018, I became a school administrator. As most administrators would tell you, in education or otherwise, it is challenging. As a school leader, one must manage people, personalities, learn and evolve in a leading role, put out "fires" as they become apparent, and get pulled in many different directions concurrently. From July 2018 to July 2020, I worked over 10 hours each day, including weekends. I was doing everything I could to help my school sites become successful and to help students. I wanted to go above and beyond my call of duty because I loved the school, the students, and the staff members.

I was able to do all this simultaneously because I had tremendous determination, grit, goal orientation, and willingness to work hard. I was also developing time management skills and organizational skills to become more efficient and effective with balancing it all.

I am still an overwhelmingly busy person pursuing living an abundant life, but I have learned to balance my time more efficiently and effectively. I have accomplished a lot in my life, going from a humble immigrant background to being a successful middle-class mother of two, living in a fantastic community in Southern California. I give presentations and write articles to share with thousands of people to help inspire and motivate them to achieve success. I am still trying to "do it all," but with more balance!

My goal is to help readers be inspired and reflect upon their own lives to make changes as they see fit. I want to empower women everywhere to fight and pursue their dreams because they deserve it!

Organization of Chapters

Many of the tricks, tips, and strategies I learned along my journey were due to my ingenuity at balancing (the best way I could) various aspects of my life successfully and simultaneously. Chapter organization is as follows:

- In chapter 1, there is a discussion of why organization skills, efficiency, and balance are essential and necessary.

- Chapter 2 is about my errors, mistakes, and reflections from when I was in middle school and high school and their trajectory over the rest of my life.

- The remaining chapters break down the same reflections from various periods, including the college years, lessons I learned from my previous jobs, classroom teacher, and leadership.

- A checklist is at the end of each chapter for practical strategies and questions for reflection and self-development purposes.

Whether the reader is a student, an employee, a business owner, or in management, organizing, prioritizing, using time very effectively will help lead a more efficient and balanced life. Although I describe my life experiences, this book is not a memoir or a biography. Instead, it helps explain how through life experiences and situations, I have acquired skills and knowledge that I now want to pass on to others. Many of the skills learned from years ago are still applicable today and can help readers develop them, as well.

Overarching Themes

The biggest takeaways for me from my journey through life are these:

- **The top 3 to 5 values in your life must take the most amount of your time and energy to live in balance. Becoming more goal-oriented will lead to more achievement.**

- **Anyone can achieve great things and accomplish primary goals if they develop strong organizational skills to become more efficient, organized, and focused.**

- **There are many opportunities, especially for immigrant women like me, to grow and thrive in the United States. Our job is to take advantage of those opportunities that arise courageously and bravely!**

These will be discussed more thoroughly throughout the book through explanations, my own experiences, and what research reveals.

Chapter 1
Organization, Efficiency, and Balance

How does organizing lead to efficiency? How does being efficient lead to more balance in life?

Here are the definitions of the words from dictionary.com:

Organizing: To form as or into a whole consisting of interdependent or coordinated parts; to systematize

Efficiency: Accomplishment of or ability to accomplish a job with minimum expenditure of time and effort.

Balance: State of equilibrium

Using these key terms, we can agree that organizing means putting the many pieces and parts of our day into a system. In other words, if that system works well, we are accomplishing what we want to do with minimum expenditure of time and effort. Thus, there will be balance in life if we appropriately manage our time and energy!

Importance of Having Balance

When we are baking or cooking, we combine different ingredients to make the final product as good as possible. If one ingredient is too much or too little, the final product will not taste as it should be. Living a balanced life is like cooking and baking.

Figure 1: How having a balanced life is like cooking and baking

https://www.cleanpng.com/png-wedding-cake-chocolate-cake-cupcake-bakery-birthda-4419094/preview.html

Just like the ingredients of the cake, we have components that come together to constitute our lives. The elements change with our age – a younger person will not have the same features that make up their life as an older person.

Figure 2: How the ingredients of life change as we age

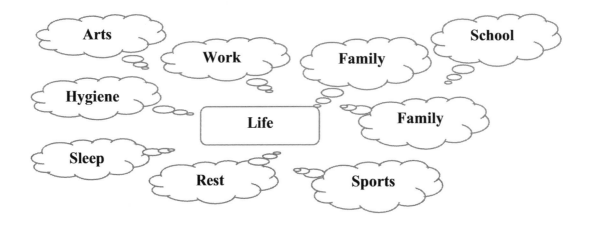

The better we put the "ingredients" of life together, the better we can live. Therefore, we need to make the most of what we can each day. Each person's priorities and values at a specific time in their lives will be the pieces that come together to make the person a whole.

When I was younger and had minimal life experience, I thought differently about how a person should live. I observed celebrities like Michael Jordan, Beyonce, and Kobe Bryant did that in their lives; they spent most of their day absorbed with that one aspect of their lives – playing basketball, performing on stage, acting, writing, etc. I admired those celebrities and wanted to be like them.

Besides celebrities, we often look up to CEOs and presidents of large organizations because they have achieved so much in life. We tell ourselves that if we work extremely hard, exceedingly long hours, non-stop, and give everything we have to our work, we can get there, too. However, a significant number of CEOs are coming out and talking about their feelings of unhappiness, isolation, and emptiness. They give so much of their time awake to their organizations and to move up the corporate ladder that they find themselves feeling exhausted. Their other goals and dreams (other than work) go unfulfilled. Celebrities have also spoken about the grueling schedules and lack of time that have led them to the end of emotional and physical breakdowns. Cheryl Sandberg, Andy Grove, and Richard Branson are some of these celebrities. Having balance is essential.

Now that I am more experienced in life, I realize giving oneself to one aspect of life is fine, but *temporarily*. For example, spending 8 to 10 hours on academics when it's the end of the semester is alright; however, spending a lot of time throughout the day focusing on only one or two aspects of life is not okay. We have a lot to do. We have many goals and dreams that should revolve around work, fun, hobby, or studies. To live life more fully, we must pay attention to all facets of life. It is all a balancing act:

Figure 3: The balance beam of life

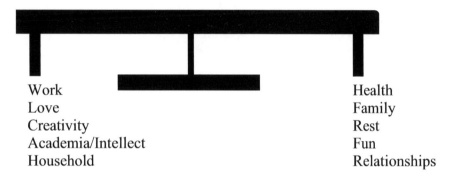

Work   Health
Love   Family
Creativity   Rest
Academia/Intellect   Fun
Household   Relationships

Fulfilling the Various Dimensions of Life

There is a wellness wheel in a book called *The New Principal's Fieldbook: Strategies for Success* that I like. The authors Pam Robbins and Alvy Harvey explain that to have balance, "one needs a balance between varieties of dimensions in life."

Figure 4: The dimensions of life

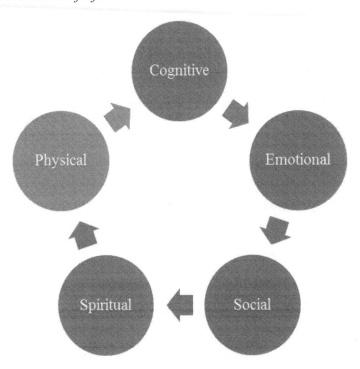

Balance in life means we give what is important to us, the aspects that we value, the most time and energy. Values and goals change with time. The number one goal on a person's list should get the most attention; the second should get the second most attention, the third should get less attention than the first two, and so on. Our lives are complicated, and we have many parts to juggle at once – work, friends, family members, finances, physical needs, psychological needs, and so on. We cannot juggle them all equally – that is not what having balance means.

It is challenging to keep balance and not let one thing in our lives overtake everything else. It's difficult not to put hours upon hours at work when we must get home to give time and energy to our families. At the same time, it's hard to provide most of our attention to just our kids and neglect other things, like work, our health, cleaning, chores, etc. It's all a balancing act.

Having balance allows us to develop relationships, spiritual growth, and creativity (Workaholics Anonymous, 2005, pg. 12). When we are well-rounded, we are open to learning and exploring new things. We become better communicators and listeners. We get more out of life and feel more content because we can learn more and enjoy what life can offer. Even colleges and universities look for well-rounded applicants when admitting students because they show more responsibility, resilience, and resourcefulness (Careervision.org, 2020). We tell high school students to be well-rounded and not just focus on academics. Colleges seek applicants who do more than just study hard for exams and do well in school; they want to see the whole person because they know who will succeed in their programs. We can live more fulfilled lives if we are better-rounded. The balancing act starts at a young age and carries forth into adulthood.

When I first became an administrator, I spent most of my day at work. I put more than 10 hours each day at the office. My job was gratifying because my actions ultimately impact the future of thousands of people. I had to think, though, about my health, my children, my husband, my desire to travel, my need to explore creativity, etc. If I were in my eighties looking back at my life, would I be able to say that I lived fully and did everything I wanted to do, or regret spending so much time at work neglecting everything else in life?

Calendaring "Life Checkpoints" Four Times Each Year

There is a practical way to stop and reflect upon life and life with balance: Using checkpoints for times each year.

Four times each year, I mark my calendar to stop and reflect on goals, needs, wants, and desires to understand if I am on the right track. I calendar for:

- January 1

- April 1

- July 1

- October 1

  I take time to go into a quiet space to think about whether my life is in balance. Here are some questions I ask myself:

- Am I spending way too much time working and not enough time on other parts of my life that are important to me?

- What are my top 5 values and priorities right now?

- Do I need to come up with goals that reflect what I want out of life?

- Do I need to be more organized with my time?

- Overall, am I efficient with the use of my time and energy?

- Do I need to manage my time better? If so, what strategies should I use?

- Do I need to be more financially organized?

- What are my top five goals right now, and are those tied to my values and priorities?

Reflecting and being honest with myself leads us to make positive changes and live more fulfilled. These are open-ended, conversational questions I ask myself.

Most of us are busy and can never stop and think about important life questions. So why not make an appointment with ourselves? Let's mark our calendars four times each year to stop and think – have a life checkpoint! If we use the Life Checkpoints, we can ask ourselves the same questions and even add some more!

Balanced Life Leads to Happiness

I have read many of the books written by Brian Tracy, an expert on goals, self-discipline, and success. He explains happiness in terms of five ingredients:

- Health and energy

- Happy relationships

- Meaningful work

- Financial independence

- Self-actualization

The idea is to consider the list and figure out where we are in each area to achieve complete happiness through self-actualization. We need to have clarity, goals based on values, an organized and efficient method of living a balanced life to achieve those goals. In Abraham Maslow's hierarchy of needs, a person's full potential is felt and seen in self-actualization, the top pyramid.

Figure 5: Maslow's Hierarchy of Needs

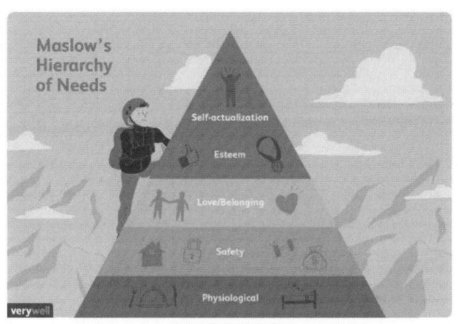

Verywell / Joshua Seong

Some of the reflective questions to ask include:

- Are my physiological needs met? Do I have proper food and shelter? If not, what goals can I set to meet those needs and move on to the other top tiers of the pyramid?

- Overall, do I feel safe in my home? Is there a financial safety net? Am I physically strong enough to continue to do the things I want to do in life?

- Am I in a loving relationship with friends, family, and my partner?

- How do I feel about myself? Am I happy with where I am in life? Do I feel successful? Have I achieved essential goals in life? Do I believe in myself and my abilities to achieve and succeed?

These are excellent reflective questions that you can ask yourself four times each year when you do the Life Checkpoints. Then, based on the responses, you can come up with clear and specific goals!

Formulating Goals Based on our Values

People's goals reflect their values, and what people value changes with time. People in their younger years have values that are very much different when they get older.

As we grow up, our family upbringing and our environment shape our values. Dictionary.com defines the word *value* as something that is of importance, worth, or usefulness. It is what a person judges as most important in life.

Reflecting upon Values that are Important to Us

It's essential to take some time and figure out what is most significant to us at whatever points we are in life. Next, we need to determine if our actions are helping us fulfill our goals toward what we value. Here are the steps to determining our core values:

1. There is a website that lists some 400 values that individuals can choose from called liveboldandbloom.com. Choose ten total.

2. We align short-term and long-term goals with our top 10 values. I prefer the following list of values:

Figure 6: My Top Ten Values

Achievement	Cleanliness
Completion	Closeness
Health	Openness
Comfort	Love
Independence	Drive

3. Look at every action taken during the day. Determine which activities take which amount of time to perform. Ask, do my daily activities align well with my values? In other words, are the things I do during the day reflect my top 10 values?

4. Alter the actions if they are not in coherence with core values. For example, if my actions and goals reflect the values shown in the figure, then chances are I'll be happy and live a fulfilled life. However, there are also values that I would not pick to be in my top 10, including:

Figure 7: My Bottom Ten Values

Assertiveness	Complacency
Meekness	Lavishness
Mysteriousness	Piety
Saintliness	Dexterity
Introversion	Coolness

In my doctoral program at the University of La Verne, the professors spent time and effort helping us figure out what our values were. After reflecting, I realized I was making progress towards my goals but not completely happy and fulfilled. Therefore, I had to make changes because my goals did not represent my values at that time.

We get fulfillment out of life when each action we take during the day validates our core values and beliefs. We need to track activities and their importance to us.

Self-discipline, Self-control, and Determination Needed to Achieve Goals

Anyone can set goals. It takes self-discipline, determination, self-motivation, grit, and a positive mindset to get them accomplished. Successconciousness.com says SELF-DISCIPLINE is self-control, avoiding unhealthy access to anything, and forgo instant gratification. In other words, we need to stop doing anything and everything that is not helping us achieve our overarching goals. Doing this takes self-discipline. Urbandictionary.com defines *determination* as simply not giving up.

Many factors play into how and why we accomplish goals, and many factors impact our inabilities to achieve some goals we set our minds to achieve. However, fear is probably the most significant and most impactful reason we do not reach our goals.

Determination, persistence, and grit are the three qualities we need to develop as we get older to achieve goals, despite significant hurdles and obstacles in life. Angela Duckworth and Lauren Eskreis-Winkler define grit as persistence over time to overcome challenges and accomplish big goals (Duckworth, 2016). If we believe in achieving and overcoming self-discipline, self-control, determination, persistence, and grit, we can achieve great things. The difficulty is controlling fear and fighting it from controlling our thoughts.

We must not succumb to fear and develop the proper mindset to succeed.

Overcoming Failures

We all have limitations, doubts, and issues with self-confidence that get in our way of thinking positively and using proactive words. Our minds are powerful instruments. When we set our minds to doing things that we feel are too hard or too impossible, we often get them done or come close to getting them done. Once we fail at something, it is easier for our brains to remind us of that failure and our inadequacy than our ability to overcome and thrive. As Richard Carlson, Ph.D., tells us in his book *Don't Sweat the Small Stuff,* "You fill your head with limitations that will frighten you from trying. The first step is to silence your greatest critic – you" (p. 119).

I find that no matter how much I want to accomplish on any given day, if I am not feeling good about my capabilities and abilities to succeed, I'm going to be out of focus. I am not going to feel well enough to accomplish and push ahead. Here are some things I have done to help myself with overcoming failures and moving forward:

- Reading and watching programs that help me with positive self-talk and self-confidence

- Looking at the actions of positive role models who have persevered in life given challenges

- Looking for "small wins" that will add up to big wins at the end

- Celebrating small successes

It is essential to have continuously read motivational, inspirational, and self-help books to keep going. Self-motivation is challenging, but we can get help from books, authors, bloggers, and people in our lives who have achieved important goals in life.

Making Progress toward Achieving the Big Goal by Celebrating Small Successes

The best way to build our sense of achievement and efficacy to achieve goals is to get small wins first. If we set a small goal and achieve it, we will be ready to take on the next bigger goal. Henry Ford once said, "Nothing is tough if you divide it into small jobs."

Having worked with adult education students in the past, I have seen this happen many times. Unfortunately, some adult learners have had little success with education and academic achievement in their histories. Yet, when they finally earn their diploma or their high school equivalency certificate, they are happy, and they get propelled to set their next goal of going to college and earning an associate's degree. One small achievement opens the door to another.

Example:

1) A person gets a job in an office doing clerical work.

2) He gets promoted after a few months to the customer service department (small win).

3) He earns a raise while working in customer service (small win).

4) He becomes the supervisor of the customer service department (small win).

5) He can move up to management but need to have some college units.

Most people can work their way up in life by achieving one small win after another. They usually stumble, though, when one of the stages requires specific skills and education that they must acquire. Nevertheless, through determination, grit, persistence, self-control, and self-discipline, we can overcome hurdles from one stage to another and get to where we want to be – financially, emotionally, and physically.

Achieve primary goals by breaking them into smaller and more manageable steps. For example, I often think of chunking in terms of preparing a large Thanksgiving meal. If I focus on each aspect individually, the pieces will all come together at the end.

Figure 8: The relationship between a Thanksgiving Meal and Major Life Goals

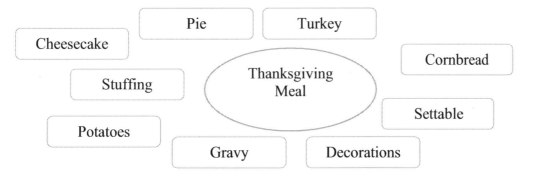

As the figure shows, if we are hosting the meal and want to make sure everything comes together smoothly and successfully, we break the large task into smaller chunks that can be achieved one at a time.

Pursuing Dreams while Managing Stress

Stress is unhealthy for the body – mentally, physically, and emotionally. When we are stressed, we make others around us miserable, whether we like it or not, because our attitude and mood are altered. I am more welcoming, warm, and friendly when I am not worried and under pressure. However, when the same people around me come to visit when tensions are high in my head, they probably leave thinking that I was upset, mean, or unapproachable. When researching stress management tips, Webmd.com has several recommendations for us (accessed 10/04/2020):

- Get enough rest or sleep.

- Seek out social support.

- Seek treatment with a psychologist or other mental health professional.

- Eat healthy, well-balanced meals.

- Make time for hobbies.

- Learn to manage time more effectively.

- Practice relaxation.

- Accept that there are events we cannot control.

- Keep a positive attitude.

  I have some other immediate means of controlling stress, which include:

- Walking away from the situation, temporarily

- Taking deep breaths

- Repeating to myself that everything is going to be okay

- Finding a private place to cry and feel better

Managing stress is difficult, but it is a natural part of everyday life. We must all learn to endure it, somehow. When we are pursuing our dreams and living toward achieving meaningful goals, stress is inevitable.

One of the biggest lessons I have learned is being self-aware. Sometimes, due to stress, I am short with my temper. However, because I am self-aware, I try to correct my behavior to ensure I am not burning bridges with those helping me in my personal and professional journeys through life.

We need to stop and reflect upon the things we do that make us happy. A friend recommended I read a book by Viktor Frankl several years ago, and I was amazed and awe-inspired by his story. Even in living through some of the worst conditions known to humankind in concentration camps, Frankl found a way to cope with his situation by being happy. One of my favorite quotes of his is, "Everything can be taken from a man but one thing: the last of the human freedoms- to choose one's attitude in any given set of circumstances, to choose one's way" (Man's Search for Meaning, 2006). We control our thoughts, and therefore our attitude toward life is governed by our feelings and thoughts. We will be filled with love and tenderness in our hearts if we choose to appreciate what we have.

Desire to Accomplish More to Live a Fulfilling Life

It is crucial to appreciate the good things we have in our lives; however, it is also essential to desire more, strive to make changes to improve our living conditions, and pursue our dreams, whatever they may be. Being appreciative does not mean being complacent and not achieving. For example, if we are unhappy with our jobs, we must see how to acquire new skills to move to other jobs and careers. We can also consider owning our own business. It's not enough to want change – we must set a specific goal and have a timeline in our minds about what steps we need to take to make them happen.

Conclusion

We all dream – especially when we are young. As we grow older and mature, our dreams become more realistic and more attainable. Our values change with time, and so do our goals. We often have goals but no concrete plans or steps on how to attain them. We must see what we want out of life and achieve those wants and desires through well-planned steps with realistic deadlines.

Here are some of the practical steps and strategies you can use to develop and progress written in the form of a checklist. Cross off each item upon completion. If you cannot cross off one of the items, think about what steps you need to take to make that happen in the next few months to few years. Those can become your short-term or long-term life goals.

☐ I have a calendar and a planner.

☐ I have marked the four days of the year when I stop and reflect upon my goals, values, and living a balanced life.

☐ I have chosen 3 to 5 primary goals that reflect different aspects of my life.

☐ I am not spending 12 hours of my day all week long focusing on one part, like work, and neglecting other things that I also want to do and achieve.

☐ Each of my primary goals has deadlines in my calendar.

☐ Each of my primary goals has five or more specific action plans.

☐ I have learned about Maslow's Hierarchy of Needs by researching articles and books to read in the next month.

☐ Once every two weeks, I will research one concept on personal development. To make sure I do not forget, I will calendar the dates to do this research.

☐ I will read 3 to 6 self-development or self-help books each year.

☐ I have written my top ten essential values and my ten least essential values.

☐ People around me during the day help encourage and motivate me to succeed in life; they push me toward becoming a better version of myself.

☐ I appreciate what I have in life, but I want to continue setting goals and achieving more. I want to get out of my comfort zone.

Chapter 2
Lessons Learned from Middle and High School that Carry Forward into Life

I was an overachieving student in middle and high school, but I cannot say I was the smartest in my classes. I was just a hard worker with a drive and determination to succeed.

My family immigrated to the United States from the former Soviet Union in late 1989 and experienced many financial hardships. Most immigrants know about the concept of living the American Dream before they even immigrate to the US. They have seen family members or friends take the big step to move to another country, a country of opportunity, and over time, find success. The keywords in that sentence are *over time*. Most people looking from the "outside" think that coming to the US means coming with no money in your pocket to having thousands, suddenly. They don't realize that, *over time*, achieving the Dream requires persistence, sweat, tears, perseverance, determination, fight, and resilience.

Like many other families, we quickly learned that having an education in the US often leads to a more secure financial future. I did not want to be poor – I did not want to live in poverty. I wanted to be financially secure, which meant I needed to go to college. I understood that college did not guarantee a more secure financial future, but that it helped! I heard the phrase "education is the great equalizer" in the United States and believed in it. It was a term coined by Horace Mann, the great pioneer of the public education system. The counselors gave good advice and guided me in my journey to pursue my dreams of going to college. The public education system believed in me.

The schoolwork was difficult for me than it should have been because of various poverty-related barriers and obstacles. I did not have the resources that other students had. I knew people in high school whose parents paid upwards of $500 to get specialized tutoring classes on weekends to prepare for SATs. Most of the students I knew had their rooms, their telephones in their rooms, as well as desks and proper learning conditions. These are physical comforts that help make a student's life easier.

There were also non-physical barriers when I was growing up. I often sat in classes and let my mind wander away – thinking about my parents' conversations about the lack of money and how they can stretch the money to make ends meet. I thought about my father's demanding working conditions as a mechanic.

Having financial difficulties gave me fuel to "keep driving" and keep fighting to achieve a better life. The system worked for me, and I owe it to my teachers, counselors, and school administrators for helping me navigate through the educational system successfully. The harder I worked in school, the more I learned and the more I enjoyed learning. I saw the fruits of my labor pay off in the form of good grades! As a result, I earned college scholarships. I used the scholarship money to pay for a laptop, books, supplies, and things that I would have had a tough time obtaining otherwise.

Being Conscious of Time

When I reflect upon my adolescent years, I remember spending so much time daydreaming instead of focusing on my work. My mind would often wander, and an assignment that should have taken 20 minutes to complete would take me 30 or 40 minutes. Over time, I had to train my brain to stop doing that by simply catching myself in the act of daydreaming and refocusing. I recently read a quote by Benjamin Franklin that said, "Do you value life? Then waste not time, for that is the stuff out of which life is made." What a powerful statement! I could have done so much more with my time had I learned to focus more. When we are conscious of how we spend time, we manage it better.

Time Management

Time management is critical and crucial to success. In his 2017 book MASTER YOUR MIND, MASTER YOUR LIFE, Brian Tracy writes, "The quality of your life is largely determined by the quality of your time management" (p. 4). Over time, the less time I wasted, the more efficient and organized I became. The trick is to be self-conscious of time – that's what I learned along the way. If we keep close track of how much time we are spending doing or not doing something, we can make the corrections necessary to refocus.

Sometimes, we know what things we do that waste time, but we do them anyway. We convince ourselves that those activities are not time wasters. How we discipline ourselves and our thoughts will change how we perceive actions and inactions.

Earl Nightingale, one of the best motivational speakers and authors of his time, once said, "We become what we think about most of the time, and that's the strangest secret." If a young person is thinking about becoming a clothing designer, most of what he does during the day ties to that vision. He will do what he can to reach that goal of becoming a designer by putting thought and effort into making the dream a reality.

I learned the value of effective time management in my adolescent years. If it wasn't for my efforts to consciously monitor my time and spend it wisely, I am sure I would not have succeeded. Some of the tricks and strategies I used to manage my time and become more efficient were:

1) Avoiding procrastination

2) Multitasking whenever possible

3) Dividing big tasks into manageable smaller chunks

4) Having organized spaces (yes, it affects time management)

5) Breaking big projects into actionable tasks

Conclusion

Now, I realize how important it is to get kids set up for the right path to success by teaching them time management skills, organizational skills, and academic skills. It is also necessary to teach them that they need to learn as much as possible to secure a better financial future and make better-informed decisions in their lives. I believe we all need to strive to be better informed and knowledgeable because being able to think for ourselves, based on our prior knowledge and experiences, will help us make better decisions for the good of everyone.

These are some of the practical steps and strategies from this chapter written in a checklist. Cross off each item as you complete it. If you cannot cross off one of the items, think about what steps you need to take to make that happen in the next few months to few years. Those can become your short-term or long-term life goals.

- ☐ For better time management, I combine at least three activities for multitasking, like studying while sitting in a waiting room or answering emails as a passenger in a car.

- ☐ I speed up completing activities that do not require much concentration, like eating or taking showers. I am carefully monitoring my daily activities to see how much time goes to each.

- ☐ I wake up 30 minutes to one hour early each day to work on goal-related tasks.

- ☐ When I have too much to do, I get help from friends and family members to focus on more essential functions.

- ☐ I have organized my desk area, my room, my drawers, cabinets, and my car to have a place for each item. Doing this will help me waste less time looking for things that I have lost or misplaced.

- ☐ I have an easel or whiteboard installed to jot down notes and important information.

- ☐ I use my phone to put in reminders (or ask my assistant to remind me of important dates and events for the day).

- ☐ I have small Post-it notes at home, kitchen drawer, car, purse, work, along with a pen or pencil, so I have writing supplies handy when needed.

- ☐ I always have my calendar nearby to job down important dates and times of events and appointments or tasks that need to get done.

- ☐ Once each week, I have it on my calendar to stop and throw away all notes, papers, and items that I know I will not need or filing them away.

- ☐ I have decluttered my home and workstations. I only have items that I actually need and use.

- ☐ Once each week, I have it on my calendar to stop and clear my email inbox, deleting items to avoid clutter. In addition, I delete voicemails as necessary to declutter my telephone memory.

- ☐ At the start of each day, I tell myself that I will stay focused and do everything I set out to do during the day.

- ☐ Since I get sidetracked quite a bit, I have set a timer to reflect upon my focus and self-discipline with getting tasks accomplished once every hour.

- ☐ On my calendar, I have set aside time each day to stop, relax, and reflect.

Chapter 3
Learning Organization Skills and Efficiency in the Early Years

It is crucial to develop organizational skills and time management skills for more efficiency in academics. The earlier people develop those skills, the better. It gets harder and harder as the student advances; therefore, the skills necessary and determination, and willingness to work hard ensure success.

My goal is to share some of the valuable lessons I gained from my earlier experiences growing up to help readers develop organizational skills and become efficient. The classes are practical and easily transferrable, no matter what the age of the reader may be!

Being able to plan effectively is a key in middle school, high school, and college. Planning allows for better time management for students who juggle a lot in their everyday lives and have various responsibilities. Planning is organizing. When a person plans, he maps out how to spend time most effectively during the day. In other words, he is "organizing" his time. Organizing time leads to more efficiency and less forgetting of when assignments are due.

Besides the regular six periods in high school, I almost always took an extra zero period class. It was hard to remember every assignment that was due. I had to develop a sound organizational system to help me stay on top of every assignment, test, and project that was due. I participated in various school clubs and organizations and checked out books to help me do well on the SATs on the weekends. I understood how vital organization was at a relatively young age and how having it together would efficiently get me through the middle and high school years.

Teaching organizational skills to kids from a very young age will set them on the right path to success. They will become task-oriented, goal-oriented, and more driven to succeed if taught how to organize effectively and efficiently.

Learning to Set Clear Goals

Setting clear goals is also a form of organization. Goals break down what we want to achieve in precise ways. They help us set expectations for ourselves and delineate the exact action steps we need to take to get there. For example, one of my goals each semester in high school was to take at least two Advanced Placement (AP) classes, take the exams at the end, and score 4's and 5's. This goal was very specific. I had to develop action plans that helped me get to those 4's and 5's after getting my AP classes. Some of those action plans were:

- Earn A's and B's to be qualified to take AP classes

- Maintain an A or B average in each class

- If grades fall below a B, get additional help from teachers and tutoring

- Plan on paying for the exams

- As exam time approaches, spend an additional 1 hour each day preparing

It is essential to be specific with academic goals or any other goals in life and write out the steps involved in achieving them. The earlier we learn how to handle forming goals, action plans, and monitoring them, the more we can achieve in life. It is best to write out specific goals with action plans because they help us stay more focused. If the action plans have a timeline or due date assigned to each, we can monitor periodically to achieve them. Prioritizing is figuring out when to accomplish each action plan or the timely step-by-step process. Setting priorities is another form of organization. We are setting practices in motion in a step-by-step manner. We know what we need to do to achieve a goal, but putting them in order of importance to complete them efficiently.

Conclusion

Some of the key lessons we learn and skills we acquire as youngsters in elementary and middle school stay with us as we grow up. The organizing skills, prioritizing, goal setting, and time-management skills help us in our daily lives and careers as we get older. The more we employ these skills, the more we will succeed!

These are some of the practical steps and strategies from this chapter written in a checklist. Cross off each item as you complete it. If you cannot cross off one of the items, think about what steps you need to take to make that happen in the next few months to few years. Those can become your short-term or long-term life goals.

☐ I have short-term goals (one year or less) and long-term goals (more than one year).

☐ I have written down goals in a journal, on a wall, or a vision board.

☐ I have specific action steps for each goal.

☐ I revise my action plans when needed.

☐ I have it marked in my calendar to review my goals once a month to make sure I am on track to meet them, usually on the first day of the month.

☐ I have an organized backpack with all items I need for easy retrieval at all times.

☐ I have my essays written at least one day before they are due so I can spend the last day reviewing and revising.

☐ I skip out on going to parties and family events if I have significant assignments due.

☐ I make sure I have extra toner for my printer so if I need to print assignments, I do not run out of ink last minute.

☐ My binder and folders for school are neat and organized.

☐ I check my grades every two days.

☐ I take breaks when I am studying for exams to recharge and get back on focus.

☐ If I do go on social media, I set a timer to make sure I can get off after ten minutes to continue to focus on my academics.

☐ I mark my calendar for having additional time for studying before finals and major exams.

☐ I have a checklist that I use to make sure all major assignments, projects, or tasks I must accomplish each week.

Chapter 4
Setting Goals and Visualizing Success

The process of setting goals is so critical to the organizational process that it is being discussed more in detail in this chapter. Brian Tracy, the bestselling author and expert on time management, says, "Before you set off on the great adventure of life, you have to decide where you want to end up" (p. 11, 2017). He explains how important it is to have clarity and a vision. Through his research and observation, he says most people go through life without any clear or concrete goals and just hope that good opportunities or resources will come their way. However, by setting some clear and concrete goals, we can follow our very own path to success. Here are examples of what it means to have clarity of goals:

- I want to get the house cleaned by 2 pm today. I envision myself sitting on the sofa when finished, the beds made, no dust anywhere, floors and carpets clean, dishes washed and put away, laundry finished.

- I want to earn a bachelor's degree in four years. I envision myself walking on stage at a graduation ceremony, feeling proud, wearing a robe, smiling, with people in the audience there to cheer for me.

- I want to lose 20 pounds in the next three months. By the end of the three months, I envision myself looking in the mirror, standing sideways, looking at the pants that I am wearing that feel much looser around my waist.

When we set the vision and mission, we write down specific ways to achieve them. The idea is not to get sidetracked on doing other activities. For example, if I am trying to get a degree, I see myself focused, attending classes in a college classroom, taking notes in a notebook, working on schoolwork late in the evenings and on weekends. If I am trying to lose weight, I see myself going out and walking for one hour each day after work, eating a small snack for breakfast, a meal at lunch that includes only vegetables, fruits, nuts, and grains. Seeing the process of accomplishing a goal in as much detail as possible is vital to achieving it.

Action plans require due dates or timelines. The only way we can monitor progress is by knowing by when we need what done. I track the progress of my goals once each month. For example, we can say we want to lose weight. How much weight? By when? We make the goal more achievable by making it measurable and assigning it a "due date." If we revise the goal to say we want to lose twenty pounds in three months, the goal becomes measurable and trackable.

It is important to note that setting goals that are too high or too outlandish can be problematic. There is a book called Organize Tomorrow Today by Dr. Jason Selk and Tom Bartow. One of the best lessons I learned from that book is how setting goals too high and hoping to "get close" can be damaging and discouraging. It can make us feel stuck, overwhelmed, and hopeless. For example, I cannot set a goal to become a WNBA player if I am 40, 5'1'', and petite in stature. This goal is unattainable since I have never played basketball before, not even in junior varsity or varsity levels in high school.

Revealing and Manifesting Goals

Writing down goals in our notebooks, planners, or even in Excel or Word documents is not only recommended but highly encouraged. Researchers state how the act of writing allows for manifestation to occur. The idea goes from our brain, through our physical being, to the outside world. The mere act of writing puts out into the universe what we want to achieve. In the first year of my doctoral program, one of my assignments was to make a vision board. Unfortunately, I did not take the vision board as seriously as I should have. The idea was to put on paper where we saw ourselves in five years. After graduating and reflecting upon my experience in the program, I realized that the idea was to get our thoughts our goals drawn out from our imaginations to become realities on paper; in other words, manifest themselves.

Types of Goals

Goals can be short-term and long-term. To achieve anything in life, we must first set a goal – whether it is an implicitly stated goal or an explicitly stated goal. Here are some short-term goals that I developed as a middle and high school student:

-Get as many straight A's as possible at the end of each semester.

-Run the mile during PE in under eight minutes by the end of the semester.

-Finish reading magazine in the backyard.

-Clean my room over the weekend.

-Watch *I Love Lucy* on television on Saturday and Sunday for one hour each day.

-Make ten meals over the weekend that can be stored and used throughout the week.

Goals Changing with Age

Our goals change as we get older. Teenagers do not necessarily have the same goals as their parents or grandparents. Our expectations, values, and needs change over time, therefore affecting our dreams and desires.

Each box below can be filled with different goals and desires, depending on where we are in life. I would argue that we have fewer goals in our early-stage and our senior stage in life.

Figure 9: Five Stages of Life

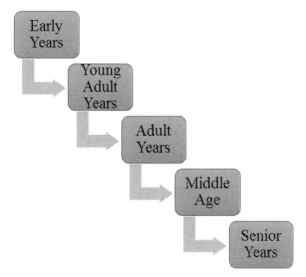

As a middle and high school student, my three overarching goals were (in order of importance from more minor to larger):

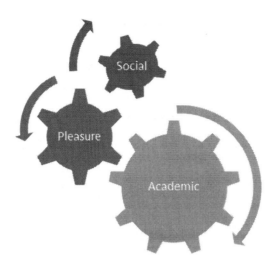

My goals as an adult all fall under the same principle categories, but the order of importance is different.

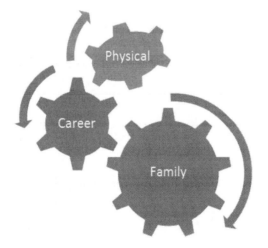

Whether planning for long-term goals or short-term goals, scheduling specific activities and planning out will help them become a reality. Most importantly, one goal will not overtake another goal – career goals will not take over physical goals, physical goals will not take over academic goals, academic goals will not take over financial goals, and so on. In other words, the plans that are important to us will all have a time and place in our planners.

Use of Planners

When I was a student, every school I attended provided me with a free planner. My appreciation for planners developed at an early age! I wrote due dates and broke down assignments into smaller chunks for each day of the week.

A planner is useless unless we actually follow through on what we set out to do each day and week. The key is to *actually do* what is written in my planner each day – not just write it and ignore it.

The more we plan for the future, the more we relieve ourselves of a great deal of stress. The more detailed our plans are, the better! We can plan our days, our weeks, and months. We can plan major events, too! Major events include:

- Weddings

- Applying for college

- Planning showers

- Planning vacations

- Planning moves from one apartment to another

- Buying a new home

- Buying a new car

Once we know our end goal, we can plan backward. For example, if we want to have a new vehicle purchased within eight months, we need to figure out what we can do each month, week, and day leading up to that point.

It is incredible how planners, schedules, and checklists can do so much to help us achieve, accomplish, and thrive.

Making Plans Based on Goals

Using the overarching goals I described earlier, I can put them in order of importance and decide how much time I should give to each activity every week.

Figure 10: Activities Associated with Particular Goals

Physical

Activities: Walk on treadmill, go for a walk at the nearby park, yoga, aerobics, tennis, swim

Total time: 6 hours per week

Career

Activities: Spend time reading books to prepare for next stage in career, search for desired future jobs and look at qualifications

Total time: 10 hours per week

Family

Activities: Take family out to dinner, watch shows together, sit and talk to kids, go to movies or shopping together, visit museums, reading together

Total time: 20 hours per week

Prioritizing Goals

I have other goals that I may not necessarily have written that I would like to devote time to each week. This is the concept of prioritizing. For example, social values are essential to me. I value my friends, family members, and people I have known for years and years. I spend 2 hours talking to old friends, neighbors or getting to know new people each week. Relaxation or pleasure is also an essential factor in my life. I spend at least one hour each day relaxing.

Sometimes we have challenges, and traumatic situations happen in our lives. Therefore, our plans get temporarily held back. Goals can be reevaluated and rewritten whenever we wish! What is essential is trkcing our brains to focus on our dreams once again.

Changing Goals and Priorities

It is also important to realize that sometimes goals can change after something a life-altering event. For example, if I find out that one of my children had a significant physical or mental diagnosis that had to be dealt with right away, my goals and priorities will alter. If there is a major natural disaster in my area, it will change my goals and priorities. If our goals are a true reflection of who we are and what we stand for, we will fight to make them a reality.

I have met many women in education who have expressed to me how much they longed all their lives to have careers but could not do so because they had to stay home to take care of their children full-time. They had to devote their time and energy to their kids' upbringing and only went back to school after the kids left the house. These women did not give up on their goals but prioritized raising their children first.

During the beginning stages of the coronavirus pandemic, I was so distraught by how little control I had over my life; I found myself spending most of my day in front of the television and eating. After two weeks of living a nightmare in my mind, I got to go back to work by my school district. Returning to work brought some "normal" back, which helped me regain some control and plan and implement goals. Sometimes we have challenges, and traumatic situations happen in our lives, and our plans get temporarily held back. What is essential is tricking our brains into focusing on our goals once again. Goals can also be reevaluated and rewritten.

Conclusion

It is never too late to set goals and write down the steps needed to achieve them within time frames.

No matter how old we are, we can continuously improve our goal setting, prioritizing, and time management skills. If there is motivation to change, we can change. We can learn skills even at a later age in life to achieve and accomplish more. Balance in life goes hand-in-hand with prioritizing, time management, organization, and efficiency.

The step-by-step process of writing and achieving goals is:

1) Identify the end goal.

2) Decide upon action plans.

3) Enter action plans into the calendar with due dates.

4) Execute action plans.

5) The goal is monitored daily, weekly, or monthly, depending on its "due date."

These are some of the practical steps and strategies from this chapter written in a checklist. Cross off each item as you complete it. If you cannot cross off one of the items, think about what steps you need to take to make that happen in the next few months to few years.

☐ I have 3 to 5 short-term goals. I have a mental picture of myself having achieved these goals.

☐ I have my 3 to 5 short-term goals in priority order, most important to least important.

☐ For each of my short-term goals, I have specific action plans and tentative dates by which I want those actions completed.

☐ I have 3 to 5 long-term goals. I have a mental picture of myself having achieved these goals.

☐ I have my 3 to 5 long-term goals in priority order, most important to least important.

☐ For each of my long-term goals, I have specific action plans and tentative dates by which I want those actions completed.

☐ I am calendaring to review and monitor my goals on the first day of every month to check my progress.

Chapter 5
Organization Skills to Achieve Goals Efficiently

Organizational skills are the keys to succeeding and realizing many goals. The more organized and efficient we are, the faster we can accomplish one goal to move on to another. We can get more out of our day, week, month, year, and life if we work and live efficiently. The trick to becoming more organized and efficient is to learn from mistakes and setbacks. We can develop these essential life skills by observing others and learning from their skills and abilities to have our systems in every aspect of our lives.

Writing Down Information to Declutter our Brains

One of my biggest peeves is when I tell myself I have to do something and not write it down because I am sure I will not forget it. Sure enough, an hour later, I know there was something important I had to do but forgot what it was. I forget because I have too much in my head to categorize and remember. I would not have this problem if I had powerful memory skills. In his book entitled *Getting Things Done*, David Allen talks about the importance of not trusting memory as an organizing system because the mind "will effectively become overwhelmed and incompetent (p. 277)." To declutter the brain, we need to write things down. Doing so will help us avoid forgetting. We can write down by:

- Using telephone voice recorders

- Emailing ourselves

- Post-it notes

- Whiteboards

- Notebooks

- Help of an assistant

We rely on our brain for intense work, and it's not meant to handle it's not equipped to handle, he says. When I learned to use my planner and make to-do lists (on my phone or paper), I became much more organized.

Organizational Techniques, Tips, and Strategies

Besides decluttering our brains, we must declutter and organize our spaces. Organization does not have to cost lots of money or require a lot of energy. Instead, we can learn from others by doing some basic research, seeing what would work for our style, and sticking to them. Here are some tips and tricks I have learned from my previous jobs that I have used over the years:

- Having a large stack of pens, pencils, highlighters on any of my desks and backpacks

- Having notebooks with me to write down things that need to get done

- Other than notebooks, having paper pads

- Having an easel or whiteboard installed to jot down notes and important information

- Using a phone for reminders

- Using Microsoft Outlook to calendar tasks and events

- Having small Post-it notes at home, kitchen drawer, car, purse, work, along with a pen or pencil

- Sending an email or text to self as a reminder

- Taking a picture to remind me to do something – often texting or emailing it to myself right away

- Always having a calendar nearby to job down important dates and times of events and appointments, or tasks that need to get done

- Once each week, throwing away all tiny notes, papers, and items that I know I will not need or filing them away to declutter

- Once each week, clearing the email inbox, deleting items to avoid clutter

- Delete voicemails that have been taken care of and do not need saving

Use of Calendars

Using a calendar is one of my best tools for organization and efficiency. Kevin Kruse, a New York Times bestselling author, wrote *15 Secrets of Successful People Know About Time Management*. He has a section of his book entitled "Live Life from Your Calendar." He conducted research and found that some of the most successful people do not merely have to-do lists but rather well-kept calendars. The calendars help them use their time efficiently.

Having a year-long calendar with a place to write daily tasks and a month at a glance is amazingly helpful. When I first purchase a calendar, here is what I do:

1) Look at day-by-day items from the previous calendar to jot down things I did last year that I would want to continue to do in the next year.

2) Put some important deadlines down, like when payments are due.

3) Write the birthdays to call, text, or email to wish people I know happy birthdays.

4) Write down on which days certain reports I need to run, because as a leader in an organization, analyzing data and basing decisions off those is crucial to success

5) Put down when important due dates are of property taxes, insurance premiums, etc.

There are some things I would like to remind myself to do each day of each month. Here are some examples:

First day of each month:

Review goals

Take and bring dry cleaning

Pay bills

The fifth day of each month:

Complete personal and professional bookkeeping

The twenty-fifth of each month:

Budget for the following month

My calendar goes everywhere with me; I'm attached to it because it has helped me save quite a bit of time over the years, becoming more productive and efficient. I use only 1 "central" calendar for work and personal needs to have everything in one place. I typically purchase an 8" by 10" booklet that I can easily carry in my purse or laptop bag.

Using the calendar of Microsoft Outlook is also very popular. However, I use it only for work-related events. Since I have trouble merging the work and personal calendars, I use my principal paper calendar/planner at all times because it's comprehensive.

Avoiding and Limiting Procrastination

I have mostly avoided procrastination throughout most of my life, even in my teenage years. Don't get me wrong: There were times when I was on very little sleep as a student in high school and college because it was crunch time. All finals came at the same time at the middle and end of each semester. It was almost impossible to spread the work and studying that had to get done over a week. But back then, and even now, I get the majority of my work planned out to get done in chunks.

Interestingly enough, *Psychology Today* explains that procrastinators are often perfectionists. They would rather not do a project at all than not do it well. Roots of procrastination are still being studied, but psychologists have identified various drivers, including low self-confidence, anxiety, lack of structure, organization, and motivation to complete tasks. Perfectionism links to Obsessive Compulsive Disorder and other mental health issues that tie to stress, anxiety, and depression (Good Therapy, 2019). When we are perfectionists, we set our bars too high for our outputs. For example, when we write a paper and keep erasing and rewriting parts because we do not feel the work is perfect, we do not get it done in a timely fashion, if at all. For many of us, putting off the writing alleviates the short-term pain the process will take. In the long run, though, this process of procrastinating will cause mental and emotional harm. Perfectionism causes energy drainage and wasted time (Chase Harper, 2020, p. 51).

To become efficient, we must avoid procrastination as much as possible. These are some strategies I use to avoid procrastinating:

- I constantly remind myself that feeling good enough about the output is what matters – there is no such thing as a perfect output.

- I work in small time increments on projects and tasks to focus better and get the work done.

- Besides breaking into smaller time increments, I divide the task into parts and complete it in pieces. I use a planner to prioritize various features of a task.

- I set realistic daily "to-do" lists and give myself a little pat on the back when I cross off each item as completed.

- I have tried to train my brain not to put off tasks. For example, in the past, I would cook large meals and leave all the dishes to be done at the very end. I realized, though, that I was mentally drained and cranky by the time I got to washing. Little by little, I trained myself to wash as I went not to have a pile at the end. By the time I am done with cooking, so are the dishes.

- Because I am in a position where I interact with people all day, especially people who look up to me for advice and mentorship, I make sure I live by what I preach. If I do things efficiently and avoid procrastination, I will inspire others around me to do the same.

Avoiding Actions and Inactions that Might Lead to Regret

Regretful actions and inactivities are a grave matter. One of my biggest fears is not doing something that I want to do and then regretting the choice later. So when I am making significant decisions about doing or not doing something, I ask myself, "Is not doing that going to make me feel regretful in the future?"

Regret is the reason why I am writing a book! I have wanted to do this for so long, and if I do not try it, I will regret it later when I am much older. Therefore, it is essential to consider our current actions, goals, and plans. Will not completing any of what we set out to do lead to regret and self-loathing? Can we use organizational skills to effectively and efficiently get things done? More severe forms of regret could lead us to form negative feelings about ourselves, leading to more significant problems related to anxiety and depression.

Researching Reasons for our Actions and Inactions

When I struggle with my feelings concerning lack of motivation, I tend to turn to Google and other such search engines. I often come across some pointers and suggestions that can help me lift myself and motivate me to do what I need.

Research can also help us understand ourselves better – having a lack of motivation, having a high level of stress, and finding the right self-help books can lead us on a path for self-improvement. Some research may lead to us seeking help from a healthcare professional, but most problems can be quickly resolved by understanding the reasons for our past actions and finding the path toward future actions. Once we feel motivated to achieve, we can develop the organizational skills to get things done. We can get back to work and get back to achieving!

Working Too Quickly or Too Slowly

Sometimes when a task is at hand or a project, I find I either work too quickly or too slowly on it. When I work too quickly, I make mistakes and regretfully see my final product as unacceptable that needs redoing. When I work too slowly, I spend more time on my task or project than needed, then fall behind on other necessary items to complete during the day. Here are some strategies that have helped me to learn to slow down or speed up with what I am doing:

- I set a timer. I estimate how much time it should take me to finish a task, and I put a timer on my phone. I become more focused on the task at hand to complete in the time allotted.

- I take quick breaks to allow my brain to get refreshed before beginning. For example, if the work I need to do is on the computer, I go to get a drink of water, walk around for just a few seconds, then return.

Asking others for Advice

We can all learn from others who are organized and well-managed with their workloads. We can adapt and implement their trips and tips for ourselves. It's the same concept as "Googling," except it's probably better because we formulate long-term friendships and relationships with people by asking.

I ask for advice if I observe someone doing something that I admire, especially when it comes to things like:

- Organization

- Public speaking

- Handling conflict

- Managing time

- Maintaining physical health

- Managing finances

- And more

Using Excel as an Organizational Tool

One way to get things done is by using Microsoft Excel sheets. Doing so will help us become task-oriented. I have various other Excel sheets saved on my flash drive that help me stay organized. Excel has unique functions and can be used in various industries to do mathematical and scientific calculations. In my world, I use it to:

- Write my monthly budget plans

- Write the meals I'm going to cook for the week

- Christmas gift list

- Weekly shopping list

- Books I want to read

- Birthdays of friends, family, and contacts

I also use Excel in my professional life. Initially, once I got used to the software program, I found it was tremendously helpful for me to save lists on my USB drive, naming them correctly for accessible location and quick use. I know there are most likely apps that also do an excellent job of helping people stay organized. People should use whichever program or resource works that for them. I have found Microsoft Excel works best for me because it's not web-based. It's an application program that suits my needs because I am very much accustomed to using it.

Limiting Distractions and Staying Focused for Small Periods at a Time

It is hard to limit distractions and stay completely focused. I have found that I can concentrate for about 20 minutes or so, and then my super active mind starts to wander. I jokingly say that I would rather have a very active brain than a sluggish brain! I accept this about myself and embrace it. Albert Camus, an Algerian-French philosopher, once said, "To understand the world, one has to turn away from it on occasion." So besides pondering and understanding the world around us, I often think about how nice it is to take mental breaks to get the creative juices flowing in our minds. Taking the breaks helps me stop and reflect on what I'm absorbing, so it works for me.

Conclusion

There are many other organizational tips, tricks, habits, and skills one can acquire in various walks of life. If we observe, learn, and adjust, we can become more organized and efficient with spending our time. The idea is to be open-minded to learning and developing organizational, time management, and prioritizing skills. By saying that what we do already is good enough, we are closing our minds to implementing change. By telling ourselves that we cannot learn to be organized and more efficient with time, we are, yet again, convincing ourselves that we cannot change. We must change our mindsets to learn and develop if we want to make changes. Mental and physical organization, prioritizing, and time management will lead to more efficiency. The more efficiently we do things, the sooner we can get tasks and projects accomplished to move on to others. More efficiency will lead to more achievement and balance in life.

These are some of the practical steps and strategies from this chapter written in a checklist. Cross off each item as you complete it. If you cannot cross off one of the items, think about what steps you need to take to make that happen in the next few months to few years.

- ☐ I have written down three to five tasks I tend to procrastinate on and develop a game plan for changing.
- ☐ I know the top three things that make me regret my actions and inactions.
- ☐ I am using Excel at least once each week for my personal or professional use to stay organized.
- ☐ Once a month or twice each week, I will search for articles and books on self-motivation to read for personal growth and development once each week or month.
- ☐ I reflect and know whether I work too quickly or too slowly on getting projects, tasks, or jobs completed. As a result, I have a plan to make changes to improve.
- ☐ This week, I will break a large task that needs to get done into chunks to get to it and finish it.
- ☐ I am observing organized people around me to learn from them.
- ☐ I have decluttered workstations.

Chapter 6
Skills Acquired from the College Years

Throughout the years I spent in college, whether working on my bachelor's degree, master's degrees, or doctoral degree, I always worked full-time. I worked full-time out of necessity – as is the case with many college students around the world.

When I was 17, a senior in high school, I started looking for a job. One day, an announcement was read over the intercom at Glendale High School in Glendale, California. I looked and found a clerical position for a local insurance agency. I started as a clerical employee, mostly filing papers in clients' files, but over time, my responsibilities increased. I acquired many skills while working at the agency concerning filing, organizing, and categorizing. However, the most important skill I learned was forming and maintaining relationships.

My goal is to share how some of the valuable lessons I gained from my time in college can be applied to everyone's professional and personal life. A person does not have to complete a college degree to learn these skills. They are transferrable and practical; they can be used to gain organizational and efficiency skills to use at any stage in life!

Creating and Maintaining Relationships

At the insurance agency, we received requests for documents that were urgent. For example, if a client were in escrow buying a home and needed evidence of insurance, we would get an urgent request for the documents to be sent immediately. If it was 4:55 pm and I was leaving at 5:00 pm, I would make sure to work on the form even if that meant staying past 5:00. I did it with absolute joy, especially if I had a good relationship with the client. Over time, the agency owner taught me how important it was to show care, kindness, empathy, and compassion for others because if I gave others good treatment, they would give me good treatment back.

The insurance agent right. I have survived and thrived in my personal and professional life because of relationships. There have been numerous occasions when I have called upon others for help and gotten their response immediately. Here are some ways I have found I can form relationships with others:

- Smile at people – it will give them the impression that I am an approachable person.

- I start conversations with people who sit near me by commenting on something or asking non-personal questions. Here are some conversation starter questions that have worked for me in the past:

    o *Did you get here early or just a few minutes ago? How was traffic for you?*

    o *Is this your first time at this school/event?*

    o *Are there others here with you?*

    o *How did you first find out about this event?*

    o *Do you know if we need to have some form of technology here with us? Are we going to have to use our phones or laptops at all?*

Once I have struck a conversation, I can keep it going because one thing will lead to another. Here are some conversation starter comments that I have used in the past:

    o I have shoes like yours! I wear them all the time because they are so comfortable!

    o I am feeling tired today, but I'm here anyway. I hope you are not as tired as I am!

    o I am not sure if I must silence my phone or put it away. I am not sure if I'm going to need it.

I can always talk about the venue, the location, the weather, or comment on something non-personal to start a conversation. Later, when the person sees you again, I will not be a stranger since a conversation occurs between us. Some people distrust and do not want to form relationships, no matter how hard I try. In my experience, nine out of ten people will respond well and make a connection, even for a moment.

We foster different kinds of relationships and need them to help us in our journey in life. Charlie Gilkey, the author of *Start Finishing*, describes four types of people who help build and support us, including:

- Guides

- Peers

- Supporters

- Beneficiaries

These individuals can be friends, family members, colleagues, acquaintances, and even social media followers. As human beings, we are meant to "fight battles" and "slay dragons" together; we are not supposed to go it alone. In all our favorite stories we read and movies we watch, the main character is not alone in their journey; there are always others to help him along, like Frodo in Lord of the Rings or Harry in Harry Potter stories. Even celebrities, like singers, athletes, and movie stars, would tell us how they were not alone in their journey to success. They had many guides, supporters, peers, and beneficiaries who helped them get to where they are.

Using Relationships as a Resource

As a student, especially in college, there are times when we must reach out and ask for help. It's nice to form relationships to rely on support from others. However, if we do not cultivate relationships, we will not have resources. Here are some examples of why it is essential to form, develop, and hang on to relationships:

- Jackie was looking for an accounting job. She was submitting resumes but not getting any calls back. When she told some of her friends and colleagues she was applying, her friend Rodolfo said he could help. He knew her from college. In addition, his sister worked at a firm and said she would love to introduce Jackie to her boss! In other words, Jackie was able to get an instant interview by having maintained her relationship with Rodolfo. She saved a lot of time and energy because rather than sending resumes blindly and awaiting calls, she managed to get an interview for a job she wanted through an old friend's connection.

- Joanna worked at Mimi's Café about 15 years ago. Even though she left, she still maintained her friendships with some of her coworkers. Angie was one of her friends. She stayed with the Café and eventually became manager. When Joanna's son was having a fundraiser at school, Joanna needed a gift basket donation. She called Angie and got three large baskets donated from the Café! Joanna would have wasted lots of time calling around asking for donations. Thanks to her friend, she saved time, energy, and stress!

- Because Jonathan knew Marvin for over twenty years, he knew he could trust him to do work for him around his house. Marvin was a contractor. Jonathan needed to replace windows. Due to the trusted relationship, he took his entire family on a weekend getaway. When Marvin came back home, all the windows were replaced! Because of his relationship with Marvin, he got an excellent price, peace of mind, and time with his family to rest and have fun while working. Imagine when it would have taken Jonathan to get quotes from contractors if it were not for Marvin!

- Tracie knew Elizabeth as her son's teacher. They had spoken on several occasions before. Thus, there was a professional relationship established. Tracie decided to ask Elizabeth what the process was like to become a teacher. She had her bachelor's degree and often wondered what she would need to do to become a classroom teacher. Elizabeth helped guide her to help Tracie realize her own goal.

We cannot have friends and formulate relationships for the sake of getting favors from them, of course. But the more people we know and more connections we have, the more prosperous we feel because we have a support system. We have reliable people around us who can help support us and talk to us. We will not be alone.

To get a lot done in a short period, we need help from others – we need relationships. When it comes to living efficiently, we cannot overstate effective and positive relationships with others.

During holidays, it's nice to send a quick text or connect now and then on social media to keep the relationship afloat. Unfortunately, we may never know when our paths may cross! To get things done efficiently, we rely on current and former relationships. We depend upon people who can help us make things happen quickly, so we do not have to do them ourselves.

Accomplishing Tasks

During my college years, I learned about building and maintaining relationships. I also learned how to focus on tasks to get them accomplished efficiently and promptly. My daily load was heavy because I had to work full-time and attend college full-time. Therefore, I used my time as effectively as possible. Here are some examples:

- Reading, highlighting, marking text while sitting in the passenger side of our car with my husband driving

- Making index cards to memorize facts and essential data to review, then use them to study while getting manicures and pedicures

- Reading and marking the text while sitting at the bleachers at my kids' swim practices

- Getting to school early enough to grab a coffee and a snack and work out math problems while sitting indoors or outdoors

- Sitting in the backyard while my kids are playing to do some reading

- During finals week, having sandwich ingredients or getting food from take-out restaurants to save cooking time to use for studying time

I found it beneficial to change scenery while studying to break the monotony to stay focused. I spent some time doing academic work in my room, then took it to the backyard, the living room, and the office. Breaking the monotony kept me more interested in the content that I had to learn and process in my mind, especially as the material became more and more rigorous.

Like many other college students, especially those who have to work while attending college because of financial necessity, there were nights when I was in very little sleep. What kept me going was the realization that what I was doing was just temporary. I knew that a master's degree took two years to complete. Once I finished, I knew I would have had more time in my hands. This knowledge gave me the push, or the "adrenaline rush," I needed to keep going day in and day out. Plus, the weekends were a great time to catch up with sleep and a bit more rest.

Setting Routines for Success

In college, I had a professor tell her class how she had a habit of waking up early each day to have about 20 minutes to have her coffee, read, and relax before heading to work. In addition, she told us how she had a routine that helped her stay organized each day. For example, she had a specific time when she had her lunch, ended her workday, checked emails, cooked, etc. The routines helped her stay organized and efficient because since she would wake up in the morning, she would have a pretty good idea of how her day would go and when to do specific unexpected tasks or errands.

When we become more organized, we naturally tend to develop routines for ourselves. We find that routines keep us from wasting time determining what comes next. Here are some practices that I have found to be very helpful:

- Having a neat and clean workstation before closing out each day
- Having an organized closet where items are neatly folded or hung
- Having separate bins in the laundry room where we place clothes to avoid piles everywhere and doing laundry only one designated day of the week
- Having a specific menu of what I am going to cook each day
- Having a particular time for my daily workout
- Having a specific time each Saturday or Sunday for hair care and nail care appointments
- Having set days and times when I go grocery shopping
- Getting the car and desk cleaned and organized when I have time off from work
- Having showers at specific times each day
- Doing Spring cleaning every year in April
- When doing something that requires focus, eliminating noise (closing door, if possible)
- Going to bed at a particular time each day

It's nice to break away from the same routines now and then for fun activities, especially during holidays, vacations, and weekends. However, it is nice to have set routines and procedures to stay organized and efficient with what we are doing with our time during the regular week. Having routines for ourselves helps us develop productivity and efficiency. When we have a set time, location, and manner in which we get our tasks completed, we get to them more rapidly and effectively.

Developing Systems-Thinking

Having routines is very much like having systems. Dictionary.com defines a *system* as a set of things working together as parts of a mechanism or an interconnecting network (accessed 2020). Unfortunately, most people feel buried and inundated with too much to do because they have not set up systems or routines to get things done. That was certainly the case with me until I decided that I needed to change. I needed a system. David Allen, a productivity consultant, explains a paradox that is well known but often not articulated: In this day in age, people have an enhanced quality of life, but at the same time, high levels of stress (Getting Things Done, 2015). As a result, more options and opportunities are available, thanks primarily to technological advancements; however, there are not enough organizational resources to take advantage of them.

Systems-thinking happens when we trust the parts of the mechanism or the network to get what we need to get done, done. For example, if I am a manager at a café, I am relying on various individuals to help me run it properly and bring back customers:

Figure 11: Systems-thinking in running a cafe

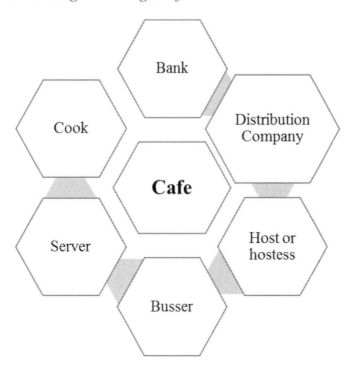

The figure above is not complete. There are more parts of the system that must work well together for the system to function correctly. If I am the café owner, I cannot rely on myself to be the busser, the hostess, the server, the cook all at the same time. Little by little, I need to bring in trustworthy helpers to get help running the business smoothly and efficiently.

The same "systems thinking" can apply to our work, academics, and our personal lives. The more we systematize and set routines, the faster and more efficiently things can get done. Systems can be applied if we look at what we do in our lives and how often we do them. Here are some examples:

- Car maintenance

- Personal care

- Grocery shopping

- Holiday decorating

- Planning celebrations or parties

- Room remodeling

After developing a system, we must monitor it. We need to analyze how well it is running periodically to make adjustments. Here are examples:

- Suppose I am a student writing a paper. In that case, I need to check every few hours or each day, depending on how close I am to being finished, what I still need to finish (pages left, research required, references, proofreading, etc.)

- If I am a business owner working on a large marketing project, I need to checkpoints to see how much has been done, how much needs to be done, and the timing and resources necessary.

- If I am an architect in a firm and I need to finish a project by a specific date, I have to check to see where I am and how much time and resources I need to complete the final project before it's due.

Often, we wait until it is too late before we make adjustments. Periodic checkpoints allow us to make small changes, so the final product comes together in a timely fashion.

Systems-thinking involves knowing the parts that come together as a whole. Thus, the organization consists of knowing what parts are needed and managing them efficiently so that the overall goal, project, or activity can come together effectively.

Systems are what help small organizations develop into larger entities. They find ways to set processes to bring more resources and expand in an organized, efficient fashion. Systems allow us to do things in organized step-by-step ways in our personal lives, academics, and professional lives. They help us achieve more in various aspects of our lives for more balance.

Conclusion

We rarely ask ourselves as we live through experiences, "How can this apply to the rest of my life?" Yet, stopping to reflect is an essential step in our journey in life. Professors did not explicitly teach many of the lessons I learned about becoming organized and efficient during my college years. Instead, there were life lessons I picked up along the way, skills I acquired that helped me then and still help me to this day.

These are some of the practical steps and strategies from this chapter written in a checklist. Cross off each item as you complete it. If you cannot cross off one of the items, think about what steps you need to take to make that happen in the next few months to few years.

- ☐ I contact two of my friends, family members, or connections to ask how they are doing every week.
- ☐ I send at least one-holiday card or greeting each year to all my contacts to let them know I remember them and care about them.
- ☐ I schedule in my calendar to do a central cleaning/organization of my workspaces and residence twice each year.
- ☐ I set a timer for how much time I spend on social media and watching television.
- ☐ I have a separate clipboard and a list for each shopping trip – Target, groceries, office supply store, Amazon, etc., so I don't have to make multiple trips to stores and save time.
- ☐ I carry a different notebook for each subject matter.
- ☐ Once a week, I save my work on a USB drive, protecting the contents of the USB drive to my laptop.
- ☐ I have a quiet area to do my job without distractions.
- ☐ I carry a pen or pencil in my purse and my car.

☐ I do a thorough cleaning and organizing of my room twice each year.

☐ I have cheap containers to store items in (paper clips, erasers, small notes, etc.).

☐ I label drawers, folders, and containers in my kitchen, closets, garage, etc.

☐ I keep extra batteries in my drawer (AAA and AA) to use for essential items that rely on them.

☐ I get rid of paperwork I know I will not need moving forward, such as old billing notices, completed assignments, etc.

☐ I set a timer for how much time I spend on social media and watching television.

☐ I have a separate clipboard for each shopping trip – Target, groceries, office supply store, Amazon, etc.

Chapter 7
Positive Mindset and Proactive Language

We are all vulnerable as human beings and susceptible to feeling inadequate when we cannot achieve what we want fast enough. We all have obstacles to overcome. Therefore, we must develop a positive mindset and use proactive language to deal with challenges and setbacks. Here is an example:

One of my goals was to be financially comfortable at the age of 40 and have a lot more disposable income to go on three or four family vacation trips each year. Unfortunately, I have not achieved this goal yet because I am still paying a bit of money on student loans each month. The two credentials, the two master's degrees, and the doctoral degree put me in a substantial financial pickle. I will probably be paying for student loans, hundreds of dollars each month, if not thousands, for the rest of my life because of my heavy debt. Having large amounts of student loans bothers me tremendously, but I try very hard to look at the positive side: I can pay the loans every month because I have a job and am doing what I enjoy in education. I cannot afford three or four trips each year; however, I can do one. Therefore, it is necessary to look at the bright side and want more for ourselves, our families, and our communities.

Developing a Positive Mindset

There has been a tremendous amount of progress made about positive and negative mindsets in recent years, brought to life by well-known authors and researchers like Carol Dweck. Her groundbreaking book, *Mindset: The New Psychology of Success*, explains that mindset is the self-perception that people hold about themselves. Dr. Dweck explains the two forms of mindsets that exist: Fixed and Growth. If a person has a fixed mindset, he will probably use phrases like, "I'll never be good in track and field because I'm not fast enough," or "I can't be a good student because I'm not like the other students who answer questions more quickly than me." On the other hand, a person with a growth mindset believes that he can accomplish great things if he tries hard and commits to his goals. In other words, a person with a growth mindset would say to himself, "All I have to do is spend a little bit more time tonight on solving systems of equations so I can do well on the chapter 8 math test tomorrow."

A positive mindset is necessary to stay mentally and physically organized and to live efficiently. Positive self-talk is essential every day to help achieve the many things that need to get done in our busy lives.

Here are some practical ideas and ways to develop and maintain a positive mindset throughout the day:

- If we are late to work or school, we tell ourselves that the rest of the day will be better – it was just a bumpy start to the day.

- If it's a cloudy day and we like sunny days, we try not to think about the clouds so much that day. Remember: Sunny days are ahead.

- If we are in an unfavorable situation, keep telling ourselves that it's temporary.

- We read articles and books on positive thinking and optimism.

- We are careful with whom we are surrounded by – others around us who are complaining and negative all the time may get us to have a negative outlook on life, too.

- If we get a low grade, we talk to the teacher to ask if we still have an opportunity to get our grade up if we work harder and earn better grades from that point forward.

- If we are upset about something, we try to distract ourselves.

- If it helps us to cry, we cry! It might help us to release the tension.

I was never the fastest reader, the most talented person in drama club, or the most athletic person in Physical Education class. However, I fought each day to get better. I learned to use proactive language and develop a growth mindset. It did not happen overnight; it took lots of self-convincing to think positively and overcome challenges. I still have to convince myself to get up and dust myself off to try again after every obstacle or challenge.

Having a growth mindset is not necessarily a skill set but a way to think to achieve things that we want. We can say we want to change something about ourselves, like becoming a better parent, better leader, better student, or better athlete. However, unless we formulate a plan and work steadily and efficiently to improve, we probably cannot get there.

Using Proactive Language

Sean Covey talks about having proactive language in his book entitled The 7 Habits of Highly Effective Teens. Much like Carol Dweck's mindset theory, he introduces teenagers to the notion of having proactive language. Dr. Covey explains the difference between a proactive and a reactive person. A reactive person may use phrases like, "There is nothing I can do," or "That's just the way it is," whereas a proactive person might say, "Let's look at other options," and "I'm going to see if there is another way." A reactive person takes power away and gives it to someone else. A proactive person takes the control back into her own hands and sees if she can change the situation for the better.

Brian Tracy, a well-known author and motivational speaker writes in his book entitled *Goals!*: "You become what you think about most of the time. Successful people think about what they want and how to get it. Unsuccessful, unhappy people think about what they don't want most of the time." We need proactive language to tell ourselves:

- We can live balanced lives and do everything we want to do in life besides just work.

- We can change our situation.

- We can be more organized.

- We can be more efficient.

- We can pursue our dreams and goals.

- I want to get more out of life.

Brian Tracy also agrees with researchers and authors of self-help books that 80% of the reasons we do not attain our goals are internal. We do not achieve because we are afraid. He suggests learning one new skill each day and practicing that skill. If we put ourselves in positions where we learn from others and acquire new skills, we will have the knowledge and ability to obtain what we did not think would be possible previously.

Disallowing Fear to Stop Us from Planning

Most people have goals and big dreams but do not work toward achieving them – even if they have the resources because of various factors. One of those factors is fear. We are afraid of failure, fearful of being judged, and afraid of hurting our egos. Fear goes hand-in-hand with a fixed mindset. It makes us think negatively about our ability to achieve.

Fear got the best of me when I was in the process of changing jobs. When I was ready to move from being a teacher to being an administrator, I planned out what I would do. My goal was to get a job in administration within six months. I wrote the following steps down in my calendar:

- Every Wednesday evening and Friday evening, search for jobs online.

- Every Thursday evening, look up videos and articles on interviewing techniques.

- Ask other administrators about their experiences to learn from them.

- On Saturdays, make five index cards of potential interview questions to practice.

- Set up one mock interview with a principal to get input on my performance.

I was following through with the plans listed above very carefully. I kept making updates to my resumes to make them more appealing and to show who I was as a leader. I kept getting interviews, but no job offers. After my sixth interview rejection, I cried and cried because I was frustrated with myself and wanted to give up. Interviewing is one of the hardest things we could do because we try so hard to showcase ourselves, and when we get rejected, we cannot help but feel inferior. Thankfully, I did not give up. I learned a little bit from each interview experience. On my 9th and 10th interviews (both on the same day, only 2 hours apart), I was offered jobs. At that point, I had to decide which one to take.

The experiences with interviewing were so tricky for me! First, I had to do some positive self-talk in my head to get myself to not feel so bad after each attempt. Second, I had to build myself up in my mind, tell myself that I could, and persist with the process. Finally, I had to develop a growth mindset.

Fear stops many people from going forward with achieving goals and dreams. By reflecting upon our experiences, thinking about what we are lacking and how we can improve, believing in ourselves and our abilities, we can make our goals a reality.

One of the biggest things I must overcome, almost daily, is fear; fear of success, fear of failure, fear of loss, fear of change.

Mark Twain has a famous quote that I think about often. He says, "Courage is the resistance to fear, master of fear – not absence of fear." He understood that we could not just tell ourselves to be fearless. Fear is one of our primal feelings that we cannot ignore. We must figure out how to work around fear and minimize its effects by taking more risks.

Conclusion

Most people go back and forth between being reactive and proactive. Most people also have a fixed mindset. If we learn to develop a growth mindset, we can do more to fight off those obstacles and barriers in our lives to make changes. We can face fear head-on! To be efficient each day, we must have a growth mindset, and using proactive language will help us climb to new heights.

These are some of the practical steps and strategies from this chapter written in a checklist. Cross off each item as you complete it. If you cannot cross off one of the items, think about what steps you need to take to make that happen in the next few months to few years.

- ☐ I will read at least one book in the next 12 months on developing a growth mindset. I will highlight sections and think about how I can use the concept to apply to my own life.
- ☐ When I make mistakes, I get upset with myself and even feel ashamed, but I remind myself that tomorrow is a new day and a new opportunity to do better.
- ☐ I reflect at the end of each day about my daily challenges and what I can do the next day differently.
- ☐ I have positive people around me who push me up.
- ☐ I plan on researching ways to overcome fear and achieve more by reading at least three books and articles in the next twelve months.

Chapter 8
Lessons Learned from Earlier Jobs Held

The jobs we do in our late teenage years and early twenties help shape our understanding of the world and the types of skills we need to acquire to move up the ladder, get promotions, or other jobs that will compensate more. Many of the skillsets revolve around having excellent people skills, critical thinking skills, and organizational skills. Those skill sets can help us go further in not just our professional lives. They can help us live more efficiently, also. The key takeaways from our earlier jobs help shape who we are in the not-so-distant future.

My goal is to share some of the valuable lessons I gained from my previous jobs and experiences that I still use today. The information will lead to gaining organizational and time management skills to use to go about things more efficiently at any stage in life!

Limiting Time Spent on Social Media

One skill I learned early on is how to use social media effectively. For young people, it is easy to be persuaded by social media posts. They get distracted several times during the day to go and look at posts on Facebook, Instagram, Twitter, and other sites while ignoring the things that must get done. I am a big fan of social media. I use it daily and love staying connecting with others. However, like everything else in life, overuse, and lack of moderation is detrimental to our chances of success.

Social media is one of the best tools today to stay connected, generate contacts, and network. It is one of the best ways to learn from others.

Over time, I have taught myself to use social media. It is not easy, so I use a timing approach. I look at social media posts in the morning for about 15 minutes and in the evening for about 15 minutes. I use a timer to remind myself that I have run out of time. There have been several times I can recall going on Facebook; then, before I know it, an hour has gone wasted that I could have spent taking care of essential tasks and daily goals. If I do not set a timer, I will spend at least an hour browsing, ignoring other responsibilities.

I started the timing method about a year ago when I realized I had to keep track of my time carefully to get more achieved. I had significant goals set for myself, like spending time with my kids, writing my book, applying for promotions, developing a website, and working on my health and well-being. Social media was a low-level priority that was taking most of my time. I needed to do something to change.

Developing Filing Skills for Everyday Purposes

Another skill I acquired in my previous jobs was developing proper filing skills. My first part-time job that became a full-time job was clerical. I wish every young person can work in a position that requires using essential organizational tools, like filing, sorting, labeling, and ordering. It will set them on the right path to success later in life. I still use some of those basic skills I learned back then in my personal and professional life today. The use of planners, Microsoft Excel, Outlook, and proper filing techniques were all organizational tools I acquired when I was in my early to mid-twenties. I learned how to apply skills to help myself become more efficient in my professional and personal life. Here are two of the strategies I use:

- At home, I have a drawer with hanging folders that have labels on them. I have one for taxes, one for the mortgage, one for each of my utility bills, telephone bills, cars, dogs, and others. Each time there is a document that I feel I might need, I properly file it in the labeled folder.

- Now that majority of bills are paid online, I receive the notices in my inbox. Once I pay, I quickly delete the message because I do not want to keep my inbox full of items that I do not need. For instance, if I need a bank statement, my banks will have my prior statements saved if I log in electronically into my account. The same is true for telephone companies, internet service providers, and others.

Drawers for Organization and Fast Retrieval

Here is a reoccurring scenario: I am looking for something, like a spice, toothpaste, or an eraser. I cannot find one of these anywhere, so I end up going to the store and buying it. A week or two later, I find I had the spice in my unorganized cabinet. I realize that I spent over $7 buying the same item unnecessarily. I overspent because of disorganization.

Situations and scenarios like the one I just described are frustrating. I have dealt with it over the years by utilizing drawers for items that I need to retrieve quickly. Looking for things can be a waste of time and, therefore, inefficient. If I can save time by organizing drawers, cabinets, and even labeling, I find I save time and money. I keep the same types of items in one location. For example, I only keep paper towels in the pantry. If I cannot find a roll there, I can't find one anywhere and must take a trip to the store. At work, I utilize one drawer for "thank you" cards, one cabinet for envelopes, one cup holder for writing utensils, etc.

Folders for Inbox and Computer Storage

What also saves me a lot of time and energy is creating folders on my USB drives. I have a few USB drives to separate items, and they are all color-coded. The one I use for personal purposes is black and contains folders like:

- Budgets

- Vacations

- Holidays

- Cooking

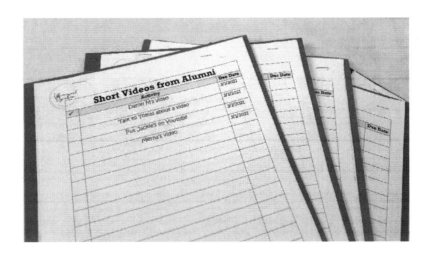

I save documents in these folders and easily retrieve them later when needed. For example, I access my budget folder once each month. In addition, I access my cooking and recipe folder once each week. I have a folder for goals. I have another folder for job finding. These folders are highly effective and efficient for me when I need to retrieve information.

Writing Emails and Memorandums More Efficiently

Some of the most effective communication skills I learned were from the jobs I held in my early to mid-twenties. Communication skills are highly sought-after by employers. Effective communication is essential in almost every line of work.

Memorandums are very formal and give no room for a personal touch. I prefer writing emails over memos because, in an email, I can start with a friendly greeting, like "Hello Mike," and ask my question or let him know what I need. I might even ask how they are doing before I proceed. Here are some ways I have found emails to be short and to the point but not lack the human element:

- Using bullets
- Disabling pop-ups
- Disabling beeps and buzzers that let me know I have a new email
- Setting up signature
- Copying & pasting messages, if needed
- Auto-responding when I'm not available
- Kindly ask the person whom I am emailing to handle my request by a specific deadline
- Keeping most emails to five sentences or less
- Having folders to store emails in only if I think I might need the item as a reference
- Unsubscribing from unwanted emails
- Having a folder for items that might take time to read, but I do not want to delete, like newsletters to read at a later time (most likely when sitting in a doctor's or dentist's waiting room)

Utilizing some or all of these strategies for organizing will save time and energy, making us more efficient and productive throughout the day. I learned many of these steps and organizational tips while working in clerical and secretarial positions while attending college.

Destroying Unnecessary Documents and Emails

I used to have piles of papers and documents on my desk at home and at work. I kept paperwork because I figured I might need them at some point. The truth is, I discovered it is a rarity to need 99.9% of those documents. I began to declutter by throwing away, shredding, and deleting.

I also delete inbox items once I have worked on them. I have seen inboxes with over 1,000 unread and read emails in them. There are people with thousands of undeleted emails in their inboxes. Most of the emails are irrelevant and unnecessary to keep, yet they clutter inboxes. I have made it a habit to delete emails from my inboxes or save the important ones in subfolders. If I think there is a slight possibility of needing something in the future, I create a subfolder to place the item there to take it out of my inbox.

Some people use the flagging method in their email inbox to mark items undone when they still need to work on them. Others have told me they keep an email unread even after reviewing it to give themselves the indication that they still need to do something further. Whatever the organization method is, keeping an inbox clear and decluttered makes way for less stress, proper prioritization, and efficiency.

Figure 12: Inbox Organization

Inbox	
Search Mail	
Compose	
Sent	
Drafts	
Deleted Items	
Spam Folder	
Folder 1 (Name)	
Folder 2 (Name)	*Use folders to save the most important emails. Name the folders for easy document retrieval.*
Folder 3 (Name)	

Seeking Perfectionism

We all want to do things as well as we can – as perfectly as possible. When we get a new job, we want to be the best we can. When we start a business, we want it to be one of the most successful out there. When we start driving, we want to be the best drivers.

Many of the young people I work with now desire to seek perfection just like I did when I was their age. When I was younger, I wanted to prove to myself and others that I was doing an excellent job and was not making any mistakes. Over time, I realized how impossible it was for me to expect to be perfect at all times and made some changes. Seeking perfection keeps us from being productive and efficient in life because nothing is ever good enough! This mindset must change for us to be able to achieve more and better outcomes in life.

To seek perfectionism but not become obsessed with it. Doing so will lead to significant emotional, psychological, and even physical problems. Some of the physical issues related to stress and worry include hypertension, heart disease, migraine headaches, depression, anxiety, chemical dependency, repetitive stress syndrome, ulcer, colitis, stress-induced asthma, shortness of breath, decreased immunity, premature labor, menstrual irregularity, impotence, teeth grinding, psoriasis, and more (Workaholics Anonymous, 2005, p. 97). We are not only hurting ourselves physically and mentally by putting excessive demands on ourselves and others around us. We are also hurting others by our demeanor, our tone, and behavior.

Part of being organized is to convince ourselves that if we make progress and get better each time, it is acceptable for things not to go as perfectly as planned. The easier we are on ourselves, the more we can accomplish because, as the saying goes, "If anything can go wrong, it will" (murphys-laws.com, 2020). Therefore, we must accept reality and do our best not to sweat the small things that will get in our way of being efficient.

Asking Questions of Others to Learn and Acquire New Skills

When I met a person with admirable qualities in my previous jobs, I always asked questions and made careful observations of their actions. For instance, if my supervisor's desk were neat and orderly, I would ask what his method of organization was so I could learn and imitate. Likewise, if a married woman had children, a job, and worked on a degree, I would ask what organizational and time management tactics she was using. Finally, if I met a female in a leadership role that I aspired to hold one day, I would look at her attire, mannerism, and personality traits to learn and adapt some of those qualities.

We need to be surrounded by people who inspire us and from whom we can learn. These individuals are our role models. We seek for qualities and characteristics that they possess to adapt and make our own! Generally, people are flattered to know that they are looked up to and admired for their actions and abilities. They are willing to help and give advice if the request is genuine and heartfelt.

Conclusion

We learn so much from those around us – we learn from their failures and successes.

It is never too late to learn from others – how they organize, manage effectively, form and keep relationships, etc. From my personal experience, people do not mind being asked to share their techniques, tips, and strategies. In fact, they see it as a compliment that someone admires their skills and wants to learn from them.

I remember pretty vividly those who have inspired and influenced me in my past. I learned by observing and imitating or by asking questions. Even now, I look for tips and strategies from others around me. For example, when I visit someone at work, I check around to see if they have certain aspects of their office that I can use myself. When I visit people's homes, I look for things that inspire me, like how they have their pantries organized, their bookshelves organized, etc. Thus, we acquire knowledge from observing, researching, and asking.

These are some of the practical steps and strategies from this chapter written in a checklist. Cross off each item as you complete it. If you cannot cross off one of the items, think about what steps you need to take to make that happen in the next few months to few years.

☐   I set a timer every time I use social media to ensure I do not spend more time on it than I have allotted each day.

☐ I have folders for my items to keep my paperwork organized and decluttered (rental agreements, school documents, tax documents, utility bills, etc.)

☐ I use drawers and cabinets to store specific items, like soap, pens, erasers, nail items, etc. If I cannot find an item I need in that particular place, I have run out and need to make a trip to the store.

☐ I have items labeled into folders on a couple of USB drives and my computer desktop.

☐ I create folders to keep only items that I might need in the future for my inbox.

☐ I unsubscribe from unwanted emails.

☐ My emails are brief and to the point.

☐ I go through and delete unwanted emails at least once each month.

☐ I observe more carefully how those around me are organizing effectively to learn from them and use their skills and tactics for myself.

☐ I catch myself spending too much time revising and overthinking things (seeking perfection).

Chapter 9
What I Learned from Being a Teacher

Teaching is a complicated and demanding job. There is a lot more to the profession than most people think.

I learned the importance of being organized when I became a new classroom teacher. A teacher cannot teach anything to a large group of students unless there is classroom management, which begins with strong organizational skills. The more organization teachers have, the better the flow is in their classrooms. Therefore, teaching is more efficient, and learning is effective.

The classroom experience I gained as a teacher is invaluable. The lessons I learned from being a teacher can apply to all other jobs and leadership positions. My goal is to share that knowledge that can apply to everyone's professional and personal life.

Having it all Together

When I was attending school, I always admired teachers who seemed to have it all together. I loved how they would have such organization, flow, and calmness about them all the time. So I aspired to be one of those teachers when it was my turn. I read a book a few years ago written by Maia Heyck Merlin called *The Together Leader* that explained what *togetherness* means:

- Prioritized
- Planned
- Efficient
- Organized
- Flexible
- Predictable
- Intentional
- Reliable

Heyck-Merlin further explains that the together leader finds "the right balance between systems and spontaneity" so goals can be met (p. 6). Organization and efficiency allow us to do everything we want to do in our personal and professional lives. Being together means having that balance between all aspects and dimensions to feel successful.

To have and keep it all together, we must have routines and procedures; in other words, systems. I learned how to establish practices and routines as a novice teacher. These routines and procedures helped us with organization and efficiency in our professional life and our personal life. We can use those same systematic ways of thinking, establishing guidelines and rules in leadership roles.

Lessons Learned in Teaching Transferred to Other Aspects of Life

In life, just like in the classrooms, we make adjustments as we go along or even change plans entirely. As long as we are staying true to our goals and values – what is important to us at that point in our lives, we do not need to be upset if changes and adjustments come our way. As a teacher, my biggest goal was to try to effectively teach in my content area so students can be well-prepared for their next level and beyond. Yes, I had a well-thought-out plan for each day, but changes and adjustments were necessary sometimes.

My lessons were organized in the same way each day, each period, which lasted approximately 55 minutes. The routines and procedures helped me tremendously with classroom management. Students also loved knowing exactly what they needed to do when they walked in because they can take control of their learning. In my fifth year of teaching, I was evaluated by my assistant principal as a distinguished teacher and even became Teacher of the Year that year. I was also a finalist in the California League of High Schools Region 10 as one of the top 10 teachers in the region.

Figure 13: Typical Class Setup

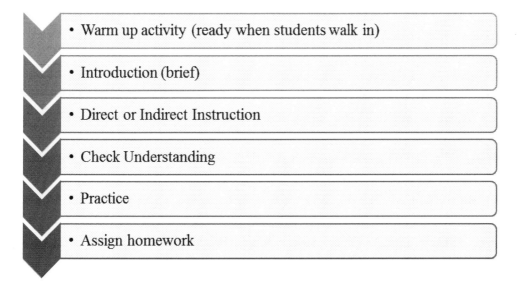

- Warm up activity (ready when students walk in)
- Introduction (brief)
- Direct or Indirect Instruction
- Check Understanding
- Practice
- Assign homework

I had my sideboard showing the daily run-down of what needed to be done, along with the essential standard I was covering. I had the homework assignments written and when to anticipate quizzes and exams.

Like in the classroom, I learned that having routines and procedures in my everyday life is essential. My children at home need procedures and practices to function effectively. The weekends are a bit more unstructured than weekdays but during the week, having routines and procedures often prevent delays and missteps.

Routines in all Aspects of our Lives

Whether we know it or not, we probably all have routines set in place because we are creatures of habit. Here are some common types of routines:

➢ Bedtime routines
➢ Chore routines
➢ Weekend routines
➢ Work routines
➢ After-work routines
➢ Morning routines
➢ Exercise routines
➢ Shower routines
➢ Study routines

➢ Travel routines

As a result of routines and structures, we can do things more efficiently, saving ourselves time, energy, and even money to use for other things in life.

Being Reflective

I learned another valuable lesson as a teacher: Being reflective. After every class, I stopped to reflect on what I should have done differently. How could I have improved the lesson? What worked well? What did not work well? For example, there was one time I was upset with a student because of his lack of desire to be in school. He was constantly interrupting me and causing havoc in the room. His behavior was out of hand. I called his mom and told her I wish he would change his schedule. I told her I did not want him in my class. I realized afterward how it must have hurt her to hear those words coming out of my mouth. After thinking about what I said that evening, I vowed to change. I decided always to be kind, empathetic, and understanding of students' social-emotional needs. I also learned how to speak when contacting parents by offering suggestions and supportive remarks on what they can do to help their kids at home.

Being reflective every day, no matter what our profession is and family life is structured, helps us become better the next day. Most of my reflection gets done either when I am alone with my thoughts. Usually, it is when I am in the shower or when I am driving. I think back on situations that occur each day and figure out how I might do it differently the next day.

Concentrating for Small Periods of Time

Another big lesson I learned from being a teacher was how to handle large tasks, like grading over 180 exams, while maintaining intense concentration. For me, it is hard to concentrate for long periods. I find that if I have to focus and concentrate on something for more than 15 minutes at a time, my mind starts to wander. I learned a few tricks as a teacher to develop better focus and concentration. For example, I chunked portions of lessons into parts. I graded papers for short periods of time so I can stay alert. I used a variety of tools to vary up the daily lessons and make things interesting.

I use similar tactics today to increase concentration. For example, I do as much as I can with a project until I notice I am losing attention and focus, then I briefly stop to work on something else. When I do speaking engagements and presentations to groups, I try to break apart and vary things up as much as possible.

Conclusion

Being organized in the teaching profession cannot be understated. Organization is vital in almost all arts and trades. Gordon Ramsay, one of my most beloved chefs, talks about the key to being organized in commercial kitchens and home kitchens all the time. Firefighters, engineers, architects, attorneys, people working in the medical profession will tell you they have systems and organizational tactics set in place to achieve success.

When there is little to no organization, and the teacher in the classroom is "winging it," students get a sense of it, and not only can havoc take over, but the loss of learning. I wish that part of the credentialing programs in colleges through the United States and beyond can include teaching organization and efficiencies as part of their curriculum to help new teachers get off on the right path to success.

Since parents are the first teachers of their children, they must teach good skills to their kids from the beginning – people skills, organizational skills, coping skills, etc. Thus, the role of a parent as a teacher and influencer is essential for a child's future.

These are some of the practical steps and strategies from this chapter written in a checklist. Cross off each item as you complete it. If you cannot cross off one of the items, think about what steps you need to take to make that happen in the next few months to few years.

- ☐ I have routines and procedures for how I operate things in my personal life and professional life.
- ☐ I have a system for doing things, but I am flexible if something unexpected occurs.
- ☐ At the end of each day, I stop and reflect on how the day went, what I could do the next day differently, and what I was proud of the most.
- ☐ I have file folders (physical and electronic) to save documents and paperwork for easy retrieval.
- ☐ I have labeled all of my folders (physical and electronic) for easy retrieval and access.
- ☐ I can quickly locate documents when I need them from my computer or USB drives.
- ☐ I have documents saved on two pieces of technology as a backup plan. For example, I save work

on my USB drive and then transfer the data to my computer at home (if the USB drive gets damaged).

☐ I carefully plan for presentations in front of groups with precise timing and information delivery.

☐ I put things away in their places every time I pick them up to avoid clutter and disorganization.

☐ My day is well-planned; I know what I will do during each hour of the day, except on days when I unplug and rest comfortably.

☐ Each night, I choose three to five main things I want to get done the following day. Planning to complete those few things gives me the motivation to wake up and get going the next day.

Chapter 10
Having Balance and Efficiency in a Leadership Position

We all find ourselves in a leadership position at one point or another. We serve in various leadership capacities in our personal lives and professional lives. Being in any leadership position could be challenging! The leader sets the tone for the team, the partnership, or the organization. Everyone looks up to them for inspiration. Influential leaders communicate well, motivate their teams, handle responsibilities well, and delegate. The leaders I look up to are those who have self-confidence, empower their staff members, and show a tremendous amount of care for their well-being. Strong leaders are organized and efficient. Having been around hundreds of people in various leadership positions, both in the private and public sectors, I have acquired some tools and ideas that have helped me become more efficient in my role in leadership.

Leaders' roles are critical to the health and well-being of hundreds, thousands, or even millions of people. A leader can be a parent, a manager, a supervisor, a teacher, a team leader, a CEO, a small business owner, a chef, a captain, a wedding coordinator, a matriarch, and more. Leaders exist in our private lives and work lives. Their roles, concerning systems-thinking and organization, are vital for the well-being of others. Their effectiveness as leaders depends on how well they can get everyone to work together for a common goal. For example, countries' leaders have teams of people to help them become organized and efficient every minute of the day. They have people who arrange their clothes for them in the morning, prepare their food, open their mail, answer correspondences, etc. They know how critical it is to have well-put-together systems around them to help them become efficient and effective in their roles.

The more leadership skills we acquire, especially in terms of time management, productivity, organization, and efficiency, the more we can succeed in our personal and professional lives.

Having an Organized Desk or Workstation

It took me time to develop the organizational skills of my physical spaces and workstations. I would misplace items, get frustrated over things I could not find, and waste time recreating documents I had already made. When I was working in the financial field, I had $300 disappear from my desktop. It was due to disarray and disorganization. My desk at work was full of paperwork stacked one on top of another. I collected $300 cash from a client that I needed to give to an appraiser. I had so much going on that day and was busy. I put the $300 somewhere on the desk to handle a phone call, fax, and answer a question for a coworker. Suddenly, the $300 disappeared. I had to pay the money out of my pocket to the appraiser for the mistake I made. I certainly could not go and ask the client to repay the money that I lost for him!

Another time, I had so much paperwork with me leaving a meeting and walking to my office that I lost an employee's timesheet. I did not turn it in by the due date, and as a result, the employee did not get compensated on time. Her timesheet got comingled with a bunch of other papers. It was due to my disorganization and lack of proper care that the employee timesheet got lost.

Since those days, I have made several changes to become more organized and better managed with my time and space. In a leadership role, especially, disorganization and disarray will lead to big problems. As leaders, we must keep things together and orderly to succeed and gain people's trust.

I often feel reluctant to give paperwork or essential documents to a person with a disorganized desk. I feel like they will lose the documents somewhere in their piles because, from experience, that has happened to me. I have lost other people's paperwork in piles and have learned my lesson. For example, I had to take my son's immunization records to his elementary school site years ago. The secretary's desk had so many piles of papers on it. She had tons of post-it notes everywhere. I gave her the copy of the records reluctantly. A day before school started, I got a call from another secretary from the school site telling me my son could not attend because I did not take in immunization records. She had misplaced the document somewhere in the piles of papers. I had to make another copy, take more time from work to go over there, and hand-deliver a copy, again!

I had a boss once tell me he purposely kept piles of files and papers on his desk to make it appear to his directors and clients that he was a very busy man. He said something so profound that I have still not forgotten it after all these years. Purposely leaving items on my desk to give a false perception is not the right way to conduct business. Some people might falsely believe that I have many documents and files on my desk because I am super busy and "in demand," but others might think I am just a disorganized person who cannot be trusted. A leader should aspire to be authentic, honest, organized, structured, and prepared at all times.

Some of the organizational techniques and strategies I have learned over the years from excellent supervisors, friends, and colleagues include:

- Once a week, cleaning up any papers or documents accumulated by shredding, filing, scanning, or delegating.

- Having the desk clear to wipe and disinfect the furniture; if covered with paperwork, dust will accumulate.

- Having items that I need for referencing in sheet protectors on the walls around my workstation or corkboards

- Having a place in the drawer for easy-to-find articles – calculators, erasers, pens, pencils, etc.

Creating Project Organizing Tools

I have tried different strategies for an organized desk, and I have finally found my million-dollar idea: pocket folders with tasks sheets stapled that I refer to as project folders. I discussed pocket folders in an earlier chapter because they have worked wonders for me. I have the tasks that need to get accomplished in a step-by-step process so I can check them off as I go. I have these nicely organized on my desk. These folders on the right side of my desk are projects or tasks that I need to work on immediately, whereas the folders on the left side are those that I need to look at a few weeks ahead. I especially like that if I cannot be at the office due to an emergency, someone else can take over and see where I am to complete the project to take over. I even use project folders for my personal needs!

There are some terrific apps and computer programs that serve the same purpose as my task sheets. Unfortunately, I am not too tech-savvy and prefer paper and pencil methods of organizing and planning. However, for people who love technology, looking into these apps and software programs is worthwhile. I make ones that are functional for me on Microsoft Word. They certainly help keep documents organized to avoid the fiasco situations I have experienced in the past with having lost paperwork and money.

Here are some suggestions for apps that have received good reviews that may be worth trying:

- Rememberthemilk.com

- Monday.com

- Dropbox

- 1password

- Trello

Keeping an In-basket on the Desk or Workstation

Rather than having documents and paperwork go anywhere on the desks and workstations, most people use an in-basket. I have an in-basket at home and work. The goal is to review the paperwork that gets delivered. I check each item, work on it, organize it by filing or discard. For example, the bills that come in the mail go in the in-basket. I love the feeling of paying them to get them done and over with and not think about them. Here are some strategies organized individuals use with in-baskets:

- Turn the in-basket upside down because the items at the bottom are the ones that came in first.

- Let everyone at home or workplace know where the in-basket is to place their documents for you there, in that one central area.

- All documents should be either thrown away, shredded or filed. They can be filed in a file folder or hanging folder in a drawer (with a label) or passed to someone else.

- After dealing with the items in the basket, they should not go back in the basket.

Having the Basic Tools for Success

Most people who do not have desk jobs have a workstation. Whether they are barbers, nail salon owners, retail shop owners, mechanic shop owners, or bakers, most people have a place where they do their paperwork. Therefore, it is essential to keep the drawers stocked with tools for organization, including:

- Stapler with staples
- File folders or hanging folders
- Post-its
- Paper clips
- Tape and tape dispenser
- Rubber bands
- Wastebasket
- Recycling bin
- Plain paper
- Notebook or notepad
- Pushpins
- Highlighters
- Scissors
- Letter-opener

Whether it is for personal organization and planning, business, or professional organization and planning, having essential tools can help with on-the-spot organization and efficiency.

Delegating Responsibilities

My favorite managers and supervisors in the past could trust and delegate work to their employees. Unfortunately, some people in leadership positions cannot delegate because they do not have enough help. Most likely, they cannot afford to have additional support within the organization. If this is the case, it is up to the leader to figure out how much work he can realistically handle. Some projects and activities may have to wait. In my second year in administration, I wanted to make so much happen for students at our site to double and triple-booked events on campus. There were huge, schoolwide and communitywide events taking place back to back. Instead of delegating each event with clear instructions and expectations, I did them myself. I spearheaded most of what was happening and created confusion along the way. It seemed that there was always something missing – either a sign-in sheet, or enough chairs in the rooms for folks to sit on, or proper signage directing traffic. The best events were the ones that were very carefully planned out with enough time ahead to slowly plan and implement over weeks, as the Multicultural Fair. Those events were also the ones where I trusted others to help me.

Once I learned to let go and give some of the big tasks to the others who wanted to gain the knowledge and experience of being in charge of events and activities, I lifted a huge load off my shoulders. As a result, I became far less stressed, which meant I was a happier person.

Charlie Gilkey, publisher, and businessperson gives the three most important reasons why handing off work to others, or delegating, fails:

- Unclear instructions

- Improper communication channels

- Someone in the process is slowing everything down

I have come across many people in management who have taken it upon themselves to do it all – either because they do not trust others or want to feel that glorious power to do it all themselves. I can admit that I was probably like that to a certain extent until I decided to make changes. As soon as I taught myself how to delegate, I became more level-headed, more efficient, and more of a motivator – what a leader should be. I get so much more satisfaction knowing that others take ownership of their work and feel like they contribute to the organization.

When having others around you help with projects or tasks, I have found it helpful to follow these basic guidelines:

Figure 14: Delegating Steps

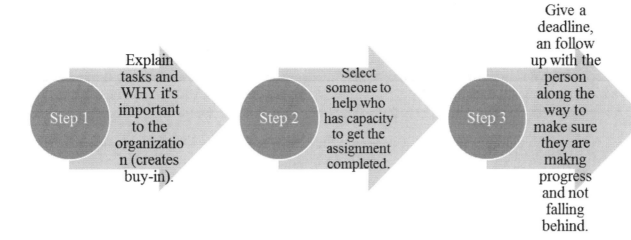

Here is a real-world example that I can draw upon from my own experience using the guide above:

Figure 15: Real-World Example of Delegating

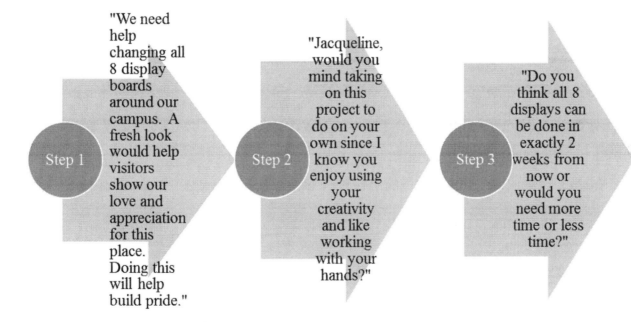

I like to give the person to whom I delegate work as much of their freedom to do the project as possible. I usually provide one or two aspects that we have to have and let them rest. In an article in the Harvard Business Review, Marion Barraud writes, "Carefully communicate any expectations for complete understanding. They can't read your mind," and he is right. Communicating effectively takes away the blame game at the end.

Delegating Work Appropriately

One of the biggest mistakes we make in leadership positions is delegating the tedious work to others because we do not want to do them ourselves. For example, suppose the tasks that require repetitiveness and boredom get passed along so as leaders, we can do the fun and exciting work. How would that make the others around them feel? Over time, it will create resentment and a lack of enthusiasm.

Delegating does not mean I have to be a boss and assign work to those who are helping. It can simply mean asking others to help – friends, family, spouses, volunteers, etc.

We must delegate work based on the strengths of the team. Some individuals have strengths that others may lack. Giving individuals the tasks that will help them shine will help boost morale! Here is one way a person in a management or supervisory position can choose to delegate work (instead of doing it themselves):

Figure 16: Delegating based on Strengths and Character Traits

Strengths and Character Traits	Type of Work Assignment
A person with excellent technology skills	• Flyer designs • Solving technology issues for peers • Providing tech help to the public • Creating documents, including meeting agendas
A person who loves talking and interacting with others	• Party-planning committee chair • Customer service support • Any type of work that is away from the computer and more interactive with the public • Train others in customer service
A person who enjoys planning ahead	• Record-keeper of calendars • Event organizer • Writer of weekly announcements

Some employees may specifically ask for certain types of work. For example, I knew someone in college who said she started working in face-to-face customer service specifically to interact with people. She was timid and introverted. She found the best way to get over the shyness was to ask her supervisor to put her in a place where she had to learn to interact with others.

The bottom line is delegating work can help the person in a leadership position use time more efficiently, thereby help the organization succeed and thrive. It will also give the leader enough time during the day to get her work done to leave and go home on time! Finally, it will allow the leader to live a more well-rounded life or a life in balance. She can focus on other aspects of her life that also need attention, like hobbies, family, home, leisure, self-development, and health.

Following up on Requests

When we allow others to help with our workload, we often give them skills and responsibilities to put on their resumes for the future. As a result, we are helping them gain knowledge, skills, experience, and self-confidence. However, people in supervisory or managerial roles must also follow up with their teams. They must check to ensure that the work is being handled quickly and accurately or intervene.

There are different hands involved in each step of the process, and more often than not, something somewhere falls apart without our knowledge. Therefore, it's best to follow up as much as possible to make sure all parts come together correctly and promptly.

Figure 17: Following up on Requests – Example

Jackie needed to order supplies from the distributor by the end of the day Tuesday.	Tuesday afternoon – check with her to see if she has ordered already or needs help getting the ordering done.
Alex needs to drive to Aaron's house to deliver a check by Friday.	Friday morning, check with Alex to see if he delivered the check or if he understands that it must get done that day.
Lucy needs to turn in her project by the end of day Saturday.	Check with Lucy on Friday to see how far along she is with completing the work. Check with Lucy on Saturday to see if she needs help getting the project completed and submitted.
Rudy needs to call the telephone company to check on the latest phone bill and get a question answered.	Check with Rudy to find out when he plans to do this. If he doesn't get back to you by the end of the day, make sure to follow up the next day.

I typically use my project folders and calendars to remember to follow up with team members.

We have to be careful with delegating too much, also. As people in leadership positions, we can trust and empower, but knowing when to stop and do something ourselves is equally important. For example, I worked for an organization where layoffs were imminent. I was a secretary at the time. Instead of sending out a memo after holding a meeting with the department leads, my boss asked me to send out the minutes I typed from the session. The minutes contained information about layoffs. As a secretary, it was not my place to break the news in that fashion to hard-working staff members who were about to see downsizing. The information should have gone out through the leader or department heads. Sometimes, it is tempting to get our assistants to help with specific tasks, but with boundaries. Proper communication can be achieved through effective organizational tactics.

Multiple Forms of Communication

Communication is one of the most critical factors for an organized, effective, productive, and efficient leader. Form and style of communication impact outcomes. There have been several times when I have wasted precious time because of my ineffective communication or lack of proper communication. For example, I ordered an installation of outdoor lighting to take place without properly informing people within the organization about it. When the technicians arrived, I was not present because of an emergency. Since no one knew what was happening, the technicians did not install, and it took ten days for them to return to my site. I wasted time and energy by my lack of communication. Even though I was embarrassed and anxious, I learned from mistakes like this. If I had communicated thoroughly, I would have been in a much better situation.

Electronic Communications

Emailing is an efficient form of communication for most people. However, not everyone reads emails thoroughly, and not everyone reads emails every hour. Moreover, people's preferences for communication are different. Some prefer email, and some prefer face-to-face or telephone communications. Others prefer printed forms and pages. Here is some information about email communications:

Figure 18: Email Communications

Long-winded emails: Because people are way too busy these days and attention spans are short, it is better to send more straightforward emails with concise language, perhaps bullets, to get to your point quickly.
Emails with no greetings: Sending an email to a coworker or an employee without a greeting may come off contemptuously. It's always best to start with hello and include the person's name for more familiarity.
Meetings with no agenda or time limits: Agendas can have one or more topics. It is best to select someone to be a timekeeper – preferably someone who has a friendly disposition and can cut off those who are not speaking concisely and using way too much time to make their point.
Emails or memos sent by secretaries: If an email or memorandum is going out, it is best to read for proper tone. Sometimes, the tone and style may come off in a condescending manner or in a way you had not intended.
Communicating in a meeting rather than an email: Sometimes, it is much better and more personable to share something in a meeting rather than an email so employees can read the leader's tone and hear the actual context of the topic
Making eye contact or greeting in hallways: We must remember that we are being looked upon for motivation and inspiration. People often take it personally and cannot help doing so if the person in a managerial position walks by and does not acknowledge their presence. They see this as an act of superiority, and it affects their self-confidence.

Stress Management

We are almost always stressed in our leadership roles because there are significant responsibilities on our shoulders. Stress management is challenging in leadership because we have to be good listeners, empathizers, and excellent non-verbal communicators. It is hard to be everything everyone wants us to be. The expectations from others are too high. Some leaders have a sound support system and can handle the stressful part of the job better than others. The less stress we experience, the better leaders we will be in every aspect of our lives. We will have less stress by managing our time effectively, building organizational skills, consistently working on our leadership skills, and becoming more efficient. By calendaring and prioritizing, we can schedule time for relaxation of the mind and body. Less stress will allow us to feel better about ourselves. Feeling more at peace will help us treat others with the utmost respect, patience, and esteem. Relationships with one another are significant. One lost opportunity to connect can take weeks and months to get back.

Using a Notebook for On-the-Go Notes

When there are many tasks to accomplish in a day, it is best to stay organized and prioritized by having a system for managing them. Some people write down tasks in order on a piece of paper. Some use post-it notes, while others use a notebook to jot down items to cross off as they complete them. Because I have had post-its get lost, I tend to use a notebook more often. For example, if I receive a phone call from someone telling me a lightbulb needs changing somewhere in the building, I write the message in my notebook. Then, as soon as the time is right, I call the maintenance department about the issue. As soon as I finish with the task, I cross it off in the notebook. I also jot down voicemail messages in my notebook to return calls. I use my notebook frequently because I have been guilty of forgetting to do things in the past. By writing them down, I have a system for remembering and prioritizing. To not lose credibility and trust with people who rely on me to help them, I must try to get to their requests and not rely on memory alone. I've found the notebook is one of the best means for me to stay organized and efficient. When I am on the go, and someone asks me for something, I send myself an email (if I have my telephone with me) or ask them to email me their request.

Prioritizing

I have often been guilty of not putting "first things first" in my professional and personal life. I have done the best I could to make adjustments to set my priorities straight. For instance, I used to obsess over how nice sign-in sheets looked for presentations. It took me at least 10 minutes to "beautify" each sign-in sheet for an event we were holding. If I calculated 10 minutes times 20 events per year, I wasted 2 hours on something insignificant.

There have been so many instances when I have caught myself doing something that was not a priority. I have had to teach my brain to stop and think about whether what I am doing is helping me achieve the most important goals of the day.

Sometimes, we all get excellent ideas. We want to drop everything and shift gears. Even though we have something we are working on, we avert our attention, effort, and time into this new idea. We often find ourselves not fulfilling goals because we are allowing ourselves to get sidetracked.

Time is finite and limited. If we are going to give time and energy to a new idea that is going to become a project, then we have to discard some other project that we were working on previously. There are only so many projects we can complete at the same time unless we had unlimited resources. Therefore, some projects and tasks need to be delegated (which means as leaders, we must trust those who are there to assist us) or discontinue altogether.

Here is how I prioritize: Today was Saturday, and I had a long list of chores and activities that needed to get done. Therefore, I have to make a quick priority list in my head as to which was an absolute necessity (based on my current goals and values, and which needed to wait either for tomorrow or next week sometime:

Figure 19: Prioritizing List

Chore or Activity	Priority (Yes or No)
2 hours on the treadmill or 6 miles	Yes
Give dog bath	No
Buy lettuce, baking soda, and spaghetti	Yes
Picking up a library book	Yes
Cooking lunch and dinner	Yes
Write a part of this book	Yes
Clean kitchen windows from the outside	No
Check on kids' homework and grades	Yes
Purchase new whisk and wooden spatulas	No

Prioritizing is an important skill set to develop. It is vital to prioritize relaxation time, as many busy, hard-working leaders forget to do.

Setting Boundaries and Personal Time Cushions

I did not quite understand the concept of boundaries and personal time until after reading some of the work of Brene Brown, a researcher, professor, and author. After reading her book, *The Gifts of Imperfection,* which was given to me as a gift by one of my mentors and professional coaches, I realized how wrong I was in not giving myself any personal time nor setting boundaries in my professional life. By not setting boundaries and personal time, I was taking away from my relaxation and family time for the sake of work.

Here are some minor adjustments I made that made me feel happier and more at peace:

- I do not listen to work-related voicemails until I am at work.

- I make a conscious effort to read work-related emails just once I get home from work and not on the weekends.

- I do not have my telephone set up to receive work emails automatically. I only check work emails when I physically log on to my work email.

Taking Productive Breaks

We need focus to be productive and efficient. Taking breaks throughout the day can help us recharge our batteries and refocus. Short breaks in-between tasks can be very helpful for our brains to stop, restore, and refocus.

Even having a few days off helps me unwind, rest my head, and think about how well I will do when I return to my everyday routines. In addition, when we take mental breaks, we tend to systematize things better, finding more organization, efficiency, and productivity.

Timely Decision-Making

As leaders, the decisions we make or do not make influence all others in the organization. It's the fear of making the wrong choice or wrong decision and looking bad that causes us to delay decision-making. Lack or delay of decision-making can cost lost money and lost time. Here are some suggestions for making decisions more rapidly and efficiently:

- Have some mentors' numbers handy to call and ask for advice when unsure what to do about a decision.

- Brainstorm ideas, especially with a team of trusted leaders, on what alternatives, and pick the best one as promptly as possible.

- Respond to requests quickly and efficiently to avoid overthinking, overanalyzing, and cluttering the brain.

- Hold yourself accountable to make decisions by writing them in your calendars and planners.

- Keep your inbox empty to avoid clutter. Doing this will also help you make decisions promptly and efficiently. After submitting a response to an email request, delete the email.

- If you need to contact someone else higher up in the organization, do so as quickly as possible.

By giving ourselves a deadline to make decisions more quickly and fearlessly, we will make determinations faster. Making swift decisions, especially when there are no moral or ethical issues involved that can be detrimental to the organization's existence, is a crucial characteristic to develop.

Conclusion

Almost every aspect of a leader's role can be done better by implementing efficiency and organization around communication, delegation, decision-making, project management, and more.

These are some of the practical steps and strategies from this chapter written in a checklist. Cross off each item as you complete it. If you cannot cross off one of the items, think about what steps you need to take to make that happen in the next few months to few years.

- ☐ Once a week, I clean up any papers or documents accumulated by shredding, filing, scanning, or delegating.
- ☐ I have my desk clear, so I can wipe and disinfect the furniture when needed. My desk is not covered entirely with files and papers.
- ☐ I have documents and policies that I need to reference sheet protectors on the walls around my workstation or corkboards.
- ☐ I have a place in the drawer for easy-to-find items – calculators, erasers, pens, pencils, etc.
- ☐ I have a system at home and at work to put incoming mail or other paperwork I need to review.
- ☐ I have a system for organizing tasks and projects in a step-by-step process using check-off lists.
- ☐ I have a system set up so that people at work will know where to pick up after me and continue in my absence if I am absent.
- ☐ I am sending a survey to my employees to answer anonymously to help me improve my leadership abilities, especially concerning trust and delegation.
- ☐ I have a system of following up with people to ensure that tasks are getting completed timely and efficiently.
- ☐ I use either a notebook, post-it notes, or a written task sheet to stay on top of tasks and assignments.
- ☐ I make a list and assign an order of priorities to the items on the list to make sure I take care of the

important things first.

☐   I do not listen to work-related voicemails until it's time to work.

☐   I make a conscious effort to read work-related emails just once I get home from work and not on the weekends.

☐   I do not have my telephone set up to receive work emails automatically. Therefore, I only check work emails when I physically log on to my work email.

☐   I take short breaks for myself to relax, unwind, and mentally refresh.

☐   I set a deadline to make decisions quickly and efficiently in my personal life and professional life.

Chapter 11
The Effects of the COVID19 Pandemic

The pandemic changed our lives tremendously. I probably would not have written this book, nor started my website or Efficiency and Organization, had it not been for the pandemic and its effects.

The Covid19 pandemic of 2019 was at its worst in late March in the U.S., early April of 2020 in the United States. In December of 2019 and January of 2020, government officials told the public that the virus was under control. However, it was too hard to stop it from spreading uncontrollably, becoming a pandemic in a few months. Many businesses were forced to close indefinitely, except for those deemed essential, like grocery stores, mechanic shops, and banks. Government officials told millions of people to work from home. Even schools were closed to in-person instruction, forcing teaching and learning to take place from home.

The pandemic forced us to slow down or stop many aspects of our lives that we deemed necessary. Even how we worked changed. For me, the sudden change in my life was so dramatic that I would say it was traumatic. For a person who is a "go-getter," always out and about, involved in the community, and overly active, being told that I had to stay home and get out of the house to only go to one or two stores was unbearable. I remember finding myself in the restroom one evening during those mid-March days and feeling an intense pressure within me. It was unexplainable. I felt bad for people I knew who were business owners and had to downsize or close their businesses. I did not know what to tell my kids and how to explain what was happening. We were entirely unprepared for a pandemic.

Taking Time to Reevaluate Goals and Values

Being permitted to go back to work after a few weeks of staying home was a relief because I felt like I had a little more control over my situation. My life was back to some "normalcy." I finally understood how organizing does not simply mean having things in neat order at home or work. That's how most people think of organizing. It means more than that. Organizing means planning, having routines, and establishing systems in every aspect of life to wisely divide up time and energy. In other words, organizing is more mental than physical. It is balancing everything we stand for in such a way to do things with efficiency and achieve more.

One of the greatest lessons I learned was how to live with balance. Before the pandemic, I spent almost my entire day awake at work. Even on weekends, when I wasn't physically at work, I took some home with me. Staying home and having more time in my hands helped me reflect upon life. "The challenge of work-life balance is, without questions, one of the most significant struggles faced by modern man," says Stephen Covey (Lifehack.org, 2020).

I also learned to prioritize my goals, values and live with more purpose in my reflections during the pandemic. I was making myself believe that everything was necessary – and everything had to be done all at once! Instead of planning and working in a step-by-step fashion, I was overexerting. Students spent much time talking about values and goals in my doctoral program. Those conversations and lessons did not hit home until the pandemic and its impact upon my life. I started backward-planning, much like teachers do when designing their content units):

Figure 20: Self-Reflecting Questions

What do I want to achieve (goals)?

Balance in Life – not spending most of my time on just one activity and neglecting other activities (changing priorities)

How do I achieve a sense of balance in my life?

Look closely at values and goals that are important to make sure every action during the day is there to make those priority goals become reality.

How do I achieve those goals and live by those values?

Organize the day, the week, the month and year in a way so to live as efficiently as possible - making time for what is important.

In every aspect of life, including health, finances, relationships, athletics, leisure, travel, child-rearing, moving, cooking, and more, we can establish systems to achieve goals efficiently.

When I started to truly value my time and not waste it as I did before, I cut the total time spent working to improve my health – both emotionally and physically. I also started to organize my time more effectively to have a balance in life.

Conclusion

I realize that disruptive, traumatic, and distressing situations are part of life that we cannot escape. The Covid19 pandemic was one of these events. Millions of people worldwide became ill, lost their jobs, livelihoods, and ultimately, their lives due to the virus.

The best way for us to analyze and make peace with what happens in life sometimes, especially unexpectedly, is to reflect and make amends – move on, but learn from what happened.

These are some of the practical steps and strategies from this chapter written in a checklist. Cross off each item as you complete it. If you cannot cross off one of the items, think about what steps you need to take to make that happen in the next few months to few years.

- ☐ I have narrowed down my list of top 10 values and beliefs. I have visited jamesclear.com/core-values to see the list of 50 values and beliefs to pick from the list.
- ☐ My goals in life are all based on my top 10 values and beliefs.
- ☐ I have a well-balanced system that incorporates all my values and beliefs into my daily activities.

Chapter 12
Organization and Efficiency in our Personal Lives

I was always so focused on work before. I had forgotten how to live and enjoy some of the other facets of my life. I was constantly in a hurry to get tasks accomplished, some of which could have been delegated or done unnecessarily, that I had forgotten what I liked to do to help myself relax and enjoy life on a daily basis:

- Sitting in the backyard, drinking coffee, listening to my 80's music

- Reading classic novels

- Cooking food I have not prepared before

- Jigsaw puzzles

- Watching comedy shows and series

- Sitting by a fire pit

- Having some weekend wine and enjoying music

- Going on short vacation trips

- Playing tennis at a local park

- Visiting amusement parks

- Visiting local museums

- Trying different restaurants to take a variety of foods

- Reading some of my favorite magazines just for fun, like National Geographic or Bon Appetit

There were times when for over 60 days straight, I did not spend any time on myself at all. I realized that I could have enjoyed life with some more organization and efficiency. I am fortunate I did not get sick in the process of being "on the go" so much. The reflections helped me become a better decision-maker and think about changes I could make to do things in my personal life to live with more balance.

Organizing time more effectively is essential!

Getting Enough Sleep

Getting good quality sleep is good for us to function properly as human beings. By organizing, planning, and prioritizing, we can get the proper amount of sleep that we need. According to Medicalnewstoday.com (2020), an average teenager needs 8 to 10 hours of daily sleep, and adults ages 18 to 65 require a minimum of 7 hours of sleep. The benefits of getting a whole night's rest include having a finely-tuned immune system, prevention of weight gain, stronger heart, better mood, increased productivity, and improved memory (sclhealth.org, 2018). Harvard Health Publishing notes those who regularly get less than six hours of sleep per night are at a higher risk of diabetes, heart disease, stroke, cognitive decline, and maybe even death (2020).

Throughout college and my earlier careers, I got enough sleep each night to function normally the following day. In fact, between where my school was located, my job location, and my place of residence, I was driving about 100 miles per day commuting each day. I had to make sure I was getting enough sleep not to feel exhausted on the roads.

It was not until I went into a full leadership role that I started to have difficulties falling asleep because of the stress involved with my job. According to ADAA.com, stress and anxiety may cause sleeping problems or make existing problems worse (2020). More than 40 million Americans suffer from chronic, long-term sleep disorders, and an additional 20 million report sleeping problems occasionally. I am currently looking at some short-term and long-term solutions to solve my problems with falling asleep. I am learning to find ways to manage the occasional heavy stress. I am also learning to be more deliberate and plan what time I go to bed and what types of activities I do about an hour before. Here are some of the step-by-step systems I am implementing:

- Not eating a large meal at least 4 hours before going to bed
- If I watch any program at all before going to bed, I make sure it's something lighthearted, like a comedy show
- Going to bed at the same time each day
- Not checking work emails at least 4 hours before going to bed to reduce stress
- Exercising (45 minutes to 1 hour on the treadmill) every single day

We have to have organization, planning, and systems in our everyday personal lives, just as we would in our professional lives to establish helpful routines and healthier habits.

Celebration Birthdays and other Major Events

I enjoy attending celebratory events in my friends' and families' lives, such as birthdays, anniversaries, and baby showers. However, I keep track of my time when I attend. I do not mean to be rude or disrespectful, but I like to stick to a schedule. Because I am a rather busy person and want to have time for myself at the end of each day, I like to attend for just a few hours. The day has to be organized in such a way to balance the many aspects of life.

Sometimes, there are pressing events happening in our lives, and we may need to reject invitations. In college, I remember I had classmates who came to take major exams completely unprepared. Instead of carving a few hours of their time to study, they attended parties with friends or family members. Being a student in college is just for a few years – it's not for an entire lifetime. Students must curtail some of the fun activities around them to complete projects, assignments, and studying on time.

Planning and Scheduling for the Weekends

It is good to have a general plan or a schedule (if there is a lot to get done) for weekends, not just weekdays. Here are some other suggestions for ways to be more organized and efficient with accomplishing goals and tasks on weekends:

1) Hire a person who can help clean the house if financial means exist. Otherwise, get help from friends and family members.
2) Order items online to not have to drive around looking for items on the weekends, especially kitchen gadgets and household items.
3) Make a list of what you need to buy from stores so your trip can be productive (separate list for Costco or Sam's Club, groceries, pet store, etc.)
4) While getting hair-cuts or other personal care work done, answer texts and emails while sitting and waiting.
5) Set aside only about 20 to 30 minutes for social media each day.
6) Write out a menu each weekend to know what foods to prepare, order, or purchase each day of the week.
7) Get most of the cooking done on the weekends, so there is no cooking done during weekdays.

If there are 24 hours in the day, we spend 8 of those asleep. Then we have 16 hours left to do what we want to do to meet our needs, goals, and desires. Once we look at how the hours are spent based on priorities, it is easy to get into the habit of living the schedule we create each because they become routines. Here is an example of how to use the time awake:

Figure 21: Allocating 16 Hours of Time Awake

Goal 1	Highest Priority	Number of hours spent: 8
Goal 2		Number of hours spent: 2.5
Goal 3		Number of hours spent: 1.5
Goal 4		Number of hours spent: 1
Goal 5		Number of hours spent: 1
Goal 6		Number of hours spent: 1
Goal 7		Number of hours spent: 0.25
Goal 8		Number of hours spent: 0.25
Goal 9		Number of hours spent: 0.25
Goal 10	Lowest Priority	Number of hours spent: 0.25
		Total must equal16 (or however many hours we are awake)

Tasks that align highly with our goals and values should get the most of our time each day. It may be necessary to make adjustments because perhaps, 16 hours is not enough time to be awake. Maybe some goals have to take longer because we cannot give two hours to it each day. It is not an exact science. However, it is worth looking at daily activities to see whether they agree with our goals and values.

Budgeting Financially

Just as we organize our time, we must manage our personal finances. I made so many awful financial mistakes in my life that now looking back. I ask myself why and how I did what I did. I bought a car from a dealership without negotiating the price or rate. For six years, I was stuck paying over $600 per month for a vehicle for which I probably could have paid $500 per month and saved $7200. I received my paychecks and spent about half on clothes at the shopping malls. I paid over $400 for a pair of sunglasses even though I was only making $10 per hour at the time. I didn't even have the money – I asked to borrow it from a close friend to buy it and pay her later (which I did). I spent so much money on things I could not afford that by the time I was 22 years old, I had about $21,000 in credit card debt.

I am not sure why I made the mistakes I made – why I kept overspending. Perhaps it was because I grew up poor, and when I was given credit cards, I splurged. Maybe I was not taught how to spend money properly and to live within my means. Perhaps I was showing off and keeping up with others. Some of the spendings may also have been a way for me to feel better about myself – giving me a temporary boost of confidence and self-esteem.

As I got older, I learned how to spend effectively and, most importantly, save. The biggest lessons learned from all the horrible mistakes I made were 1) budgeting and 2) setting financial goals. I realized how much organization with finances and budgeting would help me save time, money, and energy.

To get organized, I created a simple Excel sheet called Personal Budget. I included twelve tabs, one for each month of the year. I put income in one column and expenses in the second column. I filled in items in each of the columns (expected income and expected expenses). The goal was to estimate as effectively as possible to have the income match the spending and savings columns. Even though savings was not exactly an expense, I did include that under the expense column. Doing this allowed me to account for money that had to be saved each month for various goals.

Figure 22: Monthly Personal Budget Form

Monthly Personal Budget			

Income		Expense	
Source:	$	Type:	$
Source:	$	Type:	$
Source:	$	Type:	$
Source:	$	Type:	$
		Type:	$
		Type:	$
		Type:	$
		Saving:	$
		Saving:	$

Total Income: [   ]   Total Expense: [   ]

Besides creating and monitoring a budget every month, I have a savings plan. I have a wish list of things that we need for our family and home. Like personal and professional goals, some of the financial goals are more important or urgent than others. Some of the goals are short-term, while others are long-term.

Figure 23: Priority Savings Goals

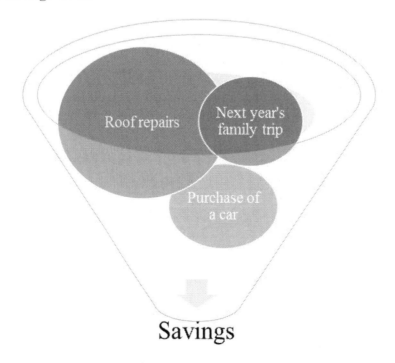

Savings

Of the three financial goals on my list, we need to have the roof repairs done soon. Because of that, more money needs to go toward that savings account every month. For example, if I can only save $200 per month, I would contribute $100 for that purpose, $60 for the family trip, and $40 to purchase a car.

I have tried different methods of becoming organized with personal finances. Using an Excel sheet worked best for me. Previously, I used Quickbooks before and Microsoft Money, along with tools provided by my credit union. I found Microsoft Excel to be the best means for me to keep things simple, organized, and efficient. What I like is each year, when I am budgeting for a new month, I can compare to the previous year to see how much expenses have increased or decreased.

Planning Vacations

We need to save for vacations and fun activities as much of a priority as possible, especially when we have families with kids. When I look back at our many years of marriage, the times that stand out in my head are the family trips we took. Some years we were on a meager budget – we could not afford big trips. We took off for a few days to go somewhere, and the entire trip cost $500 or so for a family of four. Even small local camping trips can be fun and exciting. Vacations do not need to be extravagant. As long as it's a getaway, a place to go that takes us out of the ordinary, it will help create memories that would last a lifetime. Saving for vacations is possible with organized tracking of finances and using personal budgets.

Budgeting for the Holidays

I have an Excel sheet that I use to write down the birthdays of close family members and friends to budget for gifts appropriately. I budget for holidays, as well, because doing so helps me stay organized and efficient. I used to get into debt every single year after Christmas due to overspending. I finally learned to do a better job of organizing and planning to prevent that from happening. Some of the great budgeting ideas I've picked up from people over the years include:

- Buying gifts throughout the year instead of waiting for the end of the year

- Having Secret Santa with family members to save on gifts for the whole family
- Making personalized gifts
- Baking cookies and putting them in a nice container with a note
- Saving gift cards received throughout the year to give to others on holidays
- Giving family gifts instead of individual gifts
- Saving gift wrapping to reuse in the future

Self-Discipline with Spending

Brian Tracy says, "The primary reason for financial problems in life is lack of self-discipline, self-mastery, and self-control," in his book *The Power of Self-Discipline, No Excuses!* Especially now with online shopping, it's easy to take a quick break from what we are doing to check out websites online – whether it's for home goods, clothing, jewelry, technology, etc. Buying things gives many of us instant gratification that may last for a while, but not necessarily forever.

I have personally struggled with self-discipline with saving money. I love giving myself little gifts now and then to feel better about what I am doing and where I am headed. Unfortunately, those gifts are not in my budget, and I find it hard not to spend them when I can't. One strategy that has worked for me is setting spending goals each year. I tell myself how much I can and cannot spend on things at the beginning of the year and stick to it by monitoring my spending each month.

Figure 24: Yearly Spending Limits

Type of Spending	Number of Each Item or Total Amount	Enter Date When Complete
Technology	*Upgrade telephone this year (no other tech purchases).*	
Shoes	*Purchase four pairs only this year.*	
Books	*Purchase 12 to 20 this year.*	
Kitchen	*Spend no more than $100 on kitchen items this year.*	
Food	*The monthly limit for food is $1,200 for the entire family.*	
Donations	*Limit the donations to only $250 this year.*	

By having these spending goals and limits specified, I stay on track. I teach myself self-discipline with finances by using an organized and systematic approach. I track these expenses each month to make sure I am not overspending or overbuying. This form, coupled with my monthly budget form, helps me stay on top of my finances.

Conclusion

Many successful people have organization in their personal and professional lives and have routines and daily habits. According to timecamp.com (11/23/2018), some of the most successful people from the past and the present are known to have their daily routines, notably Ernest Hemingway, Benjamin Franklin, Steve Jobs, Elon Musk, and Tim Ferriss. According to this popular blog, routines lead to better time management, self-discipline, focus, healthy balance, and more understanding.

The majority of the suggestions and tips in this chapter and the checklist come from my life experiences. To not waste time and spend my energy wisely, I had to learn to make changes. For example, I remember standing in front of the closet for 20 minutes in the morning, not knowing what to wear. I would buy blue shoes, take them home, and realize I have almost identical colors and styles in the closet. I would need to find my college transcripts and not find them because they were buried somewhere in my drawers. Over the years, I learned to be more organized to stop wasting time on what I did not want to do and instead spend that time on what I did want to do.

These are some of the practical steps and strategies from this chapter written in a checklist. Cross off each item as you complete it. If you cannot cross off one of the items, think about what steps you need to take to make that happen in the next few months to few years.

- ☐ I have a bedtime routine, such as going to bed at the same time each night, not eating a large meal a few hours before going to bed, etc.
- ☐ I have an organized plan for what I will do each day, including weekends.
- ☐ I organize my closet so outfits and articles of clothing are easy to locate.
- ☐ My pantry is organized in such a way to know where ingredients are when cooking. An organized pantry can save anywhere from 5 to 10 minutes of cooking time each day, help me to save money by not buying items I already have.

☐ I organize my garage twice each year.

☐ I use a shopping list before going shopping to save time walking around the store.

☐ I limit the amount of time I watch programs on television or on the computer to make sure other more essential tasks and activities are getting done.

☐ I donate items I do not frequently use to avoid cluttering.

☐ I go through, clean, and organize my purse or wallet every three months.

☐ If I am over my budget, I do not purchase the thing I want to get; however, I write it down for the next budget cycle.

☐ I have a list of things I need to save money for each month, and I have them prioritized from most important to least important.

☐ I have a plan and a budget for saving for gifts for birthdays and holidays.

Chapter 13
Organization, Efficiency, and Balance as a Small Business Owner

I was so proud of myself when I first opened my business, helping folks with financial matters

back in 2003. I had absolutely no money to start. I applied for a small business administration (SBA) loan

through my credit union for $15,000, and that's what it took to get going! Over time, I learned how to

develop and use organizational skills to make processes more systematic and efficient. Many of those

lessons and strategies apply to other aspects of life, not just small business operations.

When I started my small business operation, I spent about 14 hours each day, six days per week,

developing it and ensuring it was on the right path to becoming profitable. Since it was the beginning of

the journey, after about a year, I realized that the 14- or 15- hour workdays could not go on forever.

My biggest takeaway from the first year in business was finding ways to establish balance

as business owners. We must divide our time between work, family, personal development,

relaxation, and other aspects of life we value. In the beginning, the owner is expected to do it all,

including our accounting, our record-keeping, telephone answering, marketing, fixing,

maintaining, and all else associated with having a business. However, to be effective and to have

the stamina to continue without developing mental fatigue, we must set time boundaries for

ourselves and get additional help.

Effective Multitasking

I used to think that I was a terrific multitasker because I can run different activities and projects

simultaneously. However, I wasn't, exactly, multitasking. Even though I had multiple projects going on,

I was not necessarily working more than one time. In reality, I was giving each one a little bit of attention

during my day, but not concurrently.

It is possible to multitask sometimes. For example, I can fold papers while I am on the phone

having a casual discussion with someone. I can walk and talk on the telephone at the same time. I can eat while I am reading. There are ways to multitask effectively in personal and professional settings.

Figure 25: Multitasking Examples

As a business owner, if I can combine tasks, I will, as long as they do not "harm" one another.

Here are some ways to do that:

- Talk to a client on speakerphone while driving to a job site with which I am familiar

- Signing certificates while talking to the receptionist about her weekend

- Putting stamps on envelopes while listening to a marketing podcast

- Paying bills while waiting on hold on the telephone

Here are some ways I cannot multitask because the tasks simply cannot be "combined" without harming

one another:

- Talking to a client about something while emailing another client

- Having a meeting with someone face-to-face while responding to an email about something

  unrelated

- Grocery shopping while interviewing

In this list, one action affects the other action. For example, as a business owner, if I am interviewing someone while buying groceries, I am not fully engaged and attentive to what the person is saying. If I am meeting face-to-face and pretending to be taking notes on my computer, but in reality, I am checking emails, I am not fully engaged in the conversation. As long as the tasks do not need my full 100% attention to be done effectively at the same time, I can multitask. Otherwise, I am switching focus from one to the other.

Developing Consistencies and Systems

Developing consistencies and systems is fundamental to maintain organization and avoid wasted time. For example, I take my car to a nearby carwash every two months or so. I see the owner walking around and checking on the clients and employees. He asks if everyone is okay, if the employees need anything, and if the shop runs smoothly. What I love about his business is there are consistencies and systems that everyone follows. The owner has done an excellent job setting processes to start at a specific time and end at a specific time to make sure he has time for himself. He allows himself to go into his office and take care of some marketing and paperwork to rest assured that operations will continue if he is away.

We can have consistencies and systems in our personal and professional lives, not just small businesses. Systems allow us to have routines and habits that others can follow. Systems and practices help life run smoothly and efficiently. The more organization we have with our processes, the more efficiencies and the less stress. Here are some processes to systematize in small business operations:

- Client intake process

- Accounting process

- Marketing process

- Telephone answering process

- Social media process

If the processes are systems, then they can be taught to others and kept consistent. Ideally, anyone who lends a hand with the business will know what to do. Since there are systems, it will be easy to repeat steps and procedures.

When people become employed in large organizations, most of the initial stages involve teaching systems and processes. The same happens in our families. When we have guests in our homes who will stay with us for a while, we teach them the methods and systems (when we work, do house chores, go to bed, etc.). We teach children processes, like bedtime, dinner time, reading time, homework, etc.

Occasionally, it's nice to break away from routines sometimes, especially when we are on vacation or some weekends. We want the freedom to do as we wish with our time for those few days and few weeks. However, during a typical work year, the more systems and processes we have, the more organization and efficiency we will have to accomplish what we set out to do.

Sometimes in management, we do not teach or share enough knowledge due to a lack of trust. We do not think that others can do it as well as we. I had this same mentality until I saw how wrong I was not to trust others. Developing trust has to happen in small steps, incrementally. Otherwise, as small business owners, parents, educators, and employers, we get burned out by doing everything ourselves.

Surrounding Ourselves with Like-Minded People

Relationships are essential in personal and professional settings. I spent a large portion of the book discussing how much relationships can help us get to where we need to go in life to accomplish goals. Having the "right" people around us helps us convey ideas, advice, and support when in a situation. Some suggestions for ways to meet new people in business, for professional connections, or personal connections, include:

- Joining clubs

- Joining non-profit organizations

- Church groups

- Facebook groups

- Attending conferences

- Attending seminars and workshops

- Participating in leadership positions in for-profit or non-profit associations

- Following and tagging people on social media

- Linkedin groups

The more we surround ourselves with people who inspire us, the more we will improve and learn. If we want to be more productive in our lives, we have to befriend productive people! If we're going to be more organized, we have to befriend organized people. If we're going to read more and work on our self-development, we need to surround ourselves with people who have the same interests and aspirations. Being around like-minded people who have similar goals, dreams, and aspirations will push us toward success.

As small business owners, our long-term success needs to have people in our lives who can help us get through the tough days. It's essential to form relationships with other small business owners who can help us answer our questions, make suggestions, and sometimes listen to us!

Effective Use of Time

Because a small business owner juggles it all, especially in the first few years, time must be effective and efficient for the business to have any chance of survival. For example, most small businesses in their first year need to develop a clientele. They need to invest quite a bit of time in marketing and sales to produce an income. If a small business owner, like an architect, does not like marketing and sales, she may outsource that portion of the business to an outside company for a substantial fee. However, if money is tight, this may not be a viable option. Marketing can be difficult, especially if a small business owner does not necessarily have the skills or personality. The process of selling is even more difficult. Small business owners must decide the best use of their time to keep and grow the business effectively. Here is an example of how to divide up the time:

Figure 26: Example of Effective Use of Time for New Small Business Owners

Activity (in order of importance)	Time Spent
Marketing	3 hours
Customer service	2 hours
Product development or training	1 hour
Bookkeeping, billing, or accounting	1 hour
Planning	30 minutes
Other	30 minutes
Total	**8 hours**

A chart like this can be used in our personal lives and work lives, not just in small business ownership. Even students can use a chart like this to figure out their best use of time. The problem with following a system for using time effectively is self-discipline. We have to have the self-discipline to stick to the chart that we create however challenging, or even unpleasant it may be. For instance, if a basketball player is a terrific all-around player but does not know how to shoot free throws, that's where the majority of his attention and time should go during practice, right? It works the same way in our businesses, academics, jobs, and personal lives. We need to give the most time and attention to the essential activities, even if they are not the ones we want to focus on, necessarily.

Conclusion

Owning a business is extremely difficult because of the high level of stress in the first few years – especially when, as owners, we are doing it all – finances, bookkeeping, marketing, selling, ordering, organizing, and all other tasks and activities that come with the work. The faster efficiency is learned and maintained, the easier it will become to run the business.

These are some of the practical steps and strategies from this chapter written in a checklist. Cross off each item as you complete it. If you cannot cross off one of the items, think about what steps you need to take to make that happen in the next few months to few years.

☐ I have identified several systems and processes in my personal life (when I wake up, eat, groom, go to work, etc.)

☐ I surround myself with people who push me towards success and have similar interests and goals in life.

☐ I know what aspects of my life need most of my time and attention (work, small business, academics, education, home repairs, etc.)

☐ I am working on keeping in touch with my contacts and friends consistently and systematically every few months.

☐ I have a plan and a system to meet new people and form professional relationships with them.

☐ Understanding the importance of starting and maintaining relationships, I am developing new contacts, connections, and friendships.

Chapter 14
Overview of Tips, Skills, Techniques, and Ideas

We all know we have flaws and things about us we want to change. However, unless we are open-minded and willing to work on self-development, we cannot evolve and change. If we are genuinely open to learning and implementing change, even minor change, we could do it. We can make improvements in our daily lives! It is much easier to make changes when an organized system, a guide or checklist, is in place to help us. This chapter's checklist can help anyone become more organized, become more efficient, and well-managed with time to achieve more in life. Earlier chapters already contain some of these suggestions.

Here are the instructions:

1) Check off items if you are already incorporating the strategies into your day.

2) Check off items that do not apply to you.

3) Give time and attention to a technique or strategy mentioned that you could not check off immediately. For example, if you cannot check off an item having to do with Microsoft Excel, you know it's an area of need to develop.

Efficiency and Organization for Planning and Calendaring

☐ I have a planner and a calendar (paper or electronic), and I use them every day.

☐ Once each week, I have it on my calendar to stop and clear my email inbox, deleting items to avoid clutter.

☐ I have calendared four days a year to be entirely alone for a few hours. The idea is to figure out whether I am on track with my goals, needs, wants, and desires without interruptions.

☐ I have designated days in my calendar to review and monitor my goals on the first day of every month to check my progress.

Efficiency and Organization with Emails and Voicemails

- ☐ My email inbox has only a handful of emails. I delete emails I do not need or place them in folders if I think I might need to refer to something soon.

- ☐ I unsubscribe to unwanted emails immediately upon receiving them.

- ☐ I have just a few set times of the day when I check emails, so they don't distract me from doing other things that I'm supposed to do.

- ☐ I have disconnected the sound that emails make when they arrive in my inbox, so I don't get distracted by stopping from what I'm doing to check them.

- ☐ I listen to voicemails and get back to callers immediately to avoid procrastinating.

- ☐ I do not listen to work-related voicemails until it's time to work.

- ☐ I make a conscious effort to read work-related emails just once I get home from work and not on the weekends.

Efficiency and Organization with Using Technology

- ☐ I have labeled file folders (physical and electronic) to save documents and paperwork for easy retrieval.

- ☐ I can quickly locate documents when I need them.

- ☐ I have an Excel sheet called "Contacts" to keep track of people I meet at various conferences and events and not lose the relationships I build along the way.

- ☐ I use my phone to put in reminders (or ask my assistant to remind me of important dates and events for the day).

Efficiency and Organization at Home

- ☐ I have small Post-it notes at home, kitchen drawer, car, purse, work, along with a pen or pencil, so I have writing supplies handy when needed.

- ☐ I have a separate clipboard and a list for each shopping trip – Target, groceries, office supply store, Amazon, etc., so I do not have to make multiple trips to stores and save time.

- ☐ My rooms are organized, and I can easily retrieve things I need from cabinets or drawers.

- ☐ I schedule thorough cleaning and organizing of my residence twice each year.

- ☐ I have a separate clipboard and a list for each shopping trip – Target, groceries, office supply store, Amazon, etc., so I do not have to make multiple trips to stores and save time.

- ☐ I donate items that I have not used in the past two years to avoid cluttering.

☐ I have extra AAA and AA batteries on hand for my important devices.

☐ I have a pen or pencil in my purse and car for jotting down important information when needed.

☐ I have a system at home to put incoming mail or other paperwork I need to review.

☐ My closet is organized each week to pick an outfit and shoes ready to wear the next day.

☐ I use drawers and cabinets to store specific items, like soap, pens, erasers, nail items, etc. If I cannot find an item I need in that particular place, I have run out and need to make a trip to the store.

☐ I make sure there are no clutters of any kind around the house – no boxes of items around the corners, no items thrown on the floors, etc.

☐ I organize my pantry every week. I know where things are located for easy retrieving when I am cooking.

☐ I go through, clean, and organize my purse or wallet every three months.

☐ I put things away in their places every time I pick them up to avoid clutter and disorganization.

Efficiency and Organization at Work, School, or Business

☐ I have a large stack of pens, pencils, highlighters on any of my desks and in backpacks.

☐ I have notebooks (or notepads) with me to write down things that need to get done. Then, as I finish items, I cross them off on the notebook or notepad.

☐ I have organized my desk area, my room, my drawers, cabinets, and my car to have a place for each item.

☐ I have an easel or whiteboard installed to jot down notes and important information.

☐ Once each week, I throw away all small notes, papers, and items that I know I will not need or filing them away to declutter.

☐ I have a system for organizing tasks and projects in a step-by-step process using check-off lists.

☐ At the end of each day, I organize my workstation. In other words, everything has its place, and if I need a document or a supply, I can easily retrieve it.

☐ I have folders set up for ongoing projects to check/follow up with others involved in the process.

☐ I carefully observe how those around me are organizing effectively to learn from them and use their skills and tactics for myself.

☐ I have a checklist that I use to make sure all major assignments, projects, or tasks I must accomplish each week.

Efficiency and Organization by Routines and Systems

☐ I break big tasks that need to get done into chunks.

☐ I have routines and procedures for how I operate things in my personal life and professional life.

☐ I have a system for doing things, but I am flexible if something unexpected occurs.

☐ I have written down my typical weekday and weekend routines. I have written down how much each routine takes. Finally, I have reflected on what I need to change about each routine to become more organized and efficient.

☐ I have a system of following up with people to ensure that tasks are getting completed timely and efficiently.

☐ My day is well-planned; I know what I will do during each hour of the day, except on days when I unplug and rest comfortably.

☐ I only multitask when I know I can do two activities at the same time effectively.

☐ If I am absent from work, I have a system set up where others around me can quickly figure out how to help carry on my workload.

☐ I have routines set up to quit working at a reasonable hour at the end of each day to give myself a bit of time to rest.

☐ I am a routine for staying healthy.

Efficiency and Organization for Purpose, Values, and Self-Development

☐ I know what ten values are most important to me in my life. I can list them on a vision board.

☐ I am learning more about Maslow's Hierarchy of Needs by researching articles and books to read in the next month.

☐ I have healthy and happy relationships around me.

☐ People around me during the day help encourage and motivate me to succeed in life; they push me toward becoming a better version of myself.

☐ I appreciate what I have in life, but I want to continue setting goals and achieving more. I want to get out of my comfort zone.

☐ This year, I will read three self-development or self-help books.

☐ I am making health a priority and therefore changing three to five things in my life that reflect healthier living, like cutting soda-drinking, or cutting alcohol-drinking except for once a week, or limiting meat-eating to once a week.

☐ I know the top three things that make me regret my actions and inactions. However, avoiding them allows me to stay productive and motivated to achieve.

☐ I plan to attend at least one seminar or convention this year to improve myself professionally or personally.

☐ I have visited www.liveboldandbloom.com to check out the list of 400 values to make sure the ones that resonate with me are in line with my short-term and long-term goals.

☐ Once each week, I research to check out ideas on self-improvement, including:

o Time management

o Efficiency

o Organization skills

o People skills

o Developing a network

o Achieving goals

o Avoiding procrastination

o Giving up perfectionism

o Any other self-help topics

☐ I create time to reflect every single day so you can learn from my mistakes and be better the next day.

☐ I watch for signs of becoming a workaholic (spending way too much time at work to avoid going home or doing other things in my life).

☐ I am developing a positive mindset – work on thinking positively with the "I can" attitude.

☐ I use proactive language to trick your brain into thinking positively.

☐ I have snacks and plenty of water near me to eat and drink when I have a need. Having snacks and water will help with focus and hydration and allow me to work longer without taking a drawn-out break.

☐ Throughout the day, I stop and reflect at least five different times whether the work I am doing is helping me achieve the most important goals of the day.

Efficiency and Organization with Achieving Goals

- ☐ I have chosen up to 5 primary short-term goals and five primary long-term goals. Those goals reflect different aspects of my life.
- ☐ My goals in life are all based on my top 10 values and beliefs.
- ☐ Each of the goals I have come up with has a specific deadline or due date.
- ☐ I have my short-term goals in priority order, most important to least important.
- ☐ I have my long-term goals in priority order, most important to least important.
- ☐ For each of my short-term goals, I have specific action plans and tentative dates by which I want those actions completed.
- ☐ For each of my long-term goals, I have specific action plans and tentative dates by which I want those actions completed.

Efficiency and Organization with Planning

- ☐ I set a timer to avoid working on a task or project too quickly or too slowly.
- ☐ I write things down on post-it notes, my whiteboard, or my notebook to not forget to do something I have promised people I will do for them.
- ☐ I plan and attend celebratory events to show others I care and want to be present, but I plan on staying for a set amount of time due to other obligations and activities going on in my life.
- ☐ I have plans and set a schedule for weekends when I know I have a lot to accomplish.
- ☐ I plan out big projects into smaller, more manageable tasks.

Efficiency and Organization for Better Time Management

- ☐ I am working on speeding up completing activities that do not require much concentration, like eating or taking showers. I track carefully how much time goes these daily activities, then cut back minutes from each.
- ☐ I wake up 30 minutes to one hour early each day to work on specific tasks to achieve my primary goals.
- ☐ I get help on tasks and chores from friends and family members to focus on more essential functions that are helping me achieve goals (for better time management and efficiency).
- ☐ I set a deadline to make decisions quickly and efficiently in my personal life and professional life.
- ☐ I set a timer to let me know when I start working on something to finish in time.
- ☐ I set a timer for how much time I spend on social media and watching television.
- ☐ Every Monday, I look ahead to see what I have coming up to do – major events – that week and

the following week to plan accordingly.

☐ I make a list and assign an order of priorities to the items on the list to make sure I take care of the important things first.

☐ When I have something significant to accomplish to meet a deadline, I go to a quiet place where I am uninterrupted (or close the door and nicely tell everyone to understand why I have to step away).

☐ I stay on task and maintain focus for short periods.

☐ I delegate responsibility to others, even volunteers, family members, friends, and interns if possible, to learn from the experiences and grow their skill sets.

Organized Approach to Building Relationships

☐ I contact two of my connections to ask how they are doing every week.

☐ I send at least one-holiday card or greeting each year to all my contacts to let them know I remember them and care about them.

☐ When I write emails, I make sure I have a salutation. I also try to keep the emails five sentences or less for efficiency.

☐ I am on Linkedin and at least one other social media site to build connections and relationships.

☐ Understanding the importance of starting and maintaining relationships, I am developing new contacts, connections, and friendships.

☐ I have an Excel sheet where I keep track of friends, family members, acquaintances, and connections. I will use the sheet to stay in touch, send holiday cards, send well-wishes, etc.

Organized Approach to Personal Finances

☐ I have a monthly budget to keep my income and expenses balanced, giving me peace of mind knowing my spending is not out of control.

☐ I use a shopping list before going shopping to save time walking around the store.

☐ If I am over my budget, I do not purchase the thing I want to get; however, I write it down for the next budget cycle.

☐ I have a plan and a budget for saving for gifts for birthdays and holidays.

☐ I have financial goals, which are just as important as personal and professional goals.

Conclusion

There are many more strategies and techniques to be efficient, organized, and well-managed with time than what I have presented in this book. Be sure to:

1) Check off items if you are already incorporating the strategies into your day.

2) Check off items that do not apply to you.

3) Give time and attention to a technique or strategy mentioned that you could not check off immediately. For example, if you cannot check off an item having to do with Microsoft Excel, you know it's an area of need to develop.

Chapter 15
Conclusion

This book aims to provide ideas, tips, and concepts to help readers improve their lives and achieve more each and every day! I am open and honest about my challenges because I strongly value authenticity and truthfulness. Although it is uncomfortable to be open about my lived experiences, I am willing to share and become vulnerable to inspire you to overcome your challenges and persevere.

Although I have provided various ideas, ways, and means for organization and efficiency, I am still trying to improve and get better at how I manage certain things, like:

- Dealing with constant interruptions and distractions at work and home

- Giving clear instructions when delegating

- Using technology, more specifically, applications on telephones

- Making time for volunteerism

- Managing stress

- Getting enough sleep

I am still growing and discovering better ways to do things more effectively and efficiently. Despite my thorough research on the topics written in the book, I am still developing and improving.

Over the years, I have learned about organization simply by trial and error and developing ways to help myself swim and not sink quickly. Sean Covey, a well-known American author, asks his young readers to consider what heroic acts may not have taken place if the people who accomplished them acted in the face of fear (The 7 Habits of Highly Effective Teens (p.118). It is fear of failure that often stops us from accomplishing specific tasks and fulfilling goals. By establishing certain organizational measures, systems, and efficient ways to do things, we can reduce the fear of failure. We can have specific strategies in place to achieve our goals with less fear and apprehension. It's also important to be open-minded about new ways of doing things. Self-development is about being open to learning and changing.

In an earlier chapter, I discussed how important it is to be reflective. I cannot overstate the importance of reflecting at the end of each day. I mostly think back when I am driving at the end of the workday by asking myself, what would I have done differently with certain situations? Was my day productive enough? Did I meet my objectives? Did I speak to someone in a way I should not have said? Should I have managed my stress better? My thoughts usually revolve around how I spent my time – whether I need to be more focused the next day, be more relaxed, more visible, or more energetic. I make changes and adjustments each day.

Through my reflections over the years, I have learned the value of organizational skills and how they lead to efficiency. Having more efficiency means having effective time management. Proper time management leads to living a more balanced life. In *Time Management Hacks*, Andrea Chase Harper how what causes us much stress in our busy lifestyles is "a pronounced failure to effectively manage [our] time and progress in [our] career" (p. 10). She further states, "In worst cases, the stress and anxiety can lead to both serious mental and physical deterioration of health." Having a well-thought-out plan about spending the minutes and hours in our days makes a huge difference because time is finite – we cannot get any of it back. Therefore, having systems in place for being more organized and efficient with our time and energy will lead to accomplishing more goals, living purposefully, and realizing our dreams or aspirations!

It took me years to develop the organizational skills and efficiency to manage my time better. I am continuously improving and making changes just yet. However, I do want to share what I have learned so far with you as one of my beloved readers. I want to share my journey to help you achieve and thrive while living a happier, more balanced life!

References

Allen, D. (2015). *Getting things done: The art of stress-free productivity.* New York: Penguin Books.

Avidor, R. (n.d.). *Murphy's laws site All the laws of Murphy in one place.* Murphy Laws Site - Origin. http://www.murphys-laws.com/murphy/murphy-true.html.

Brown Brené. (2020). *The gifts of imperfection: let go of who you think you're supposed to be and embrace who you are.* Vermilion.

Buckingham, M. & Clifton, D. O. (2001). *Now, Discover your Strengths.* The Free Press. New York.

Burnett, B., & Evans, D. (2016). *Designing your Life: How to Build a Well-Lived, Joyful Life.* New York: Knopf, Borzoi Books.

Carlson, R. (1997). *Don't Sweat the Small Stuff...and it's all Small Stuff: Simple Ways to Keep the Little Things from Taking Over Your Life.* New York: MJF Books

Chand, MD, S. (2016, June 15). *How to Handle Regret.* Anxiety and Depression Association of America, ADAA. https://adaa.org/learn-from-us/from-the-experts/blog-posts/consumer/how-handle-regret.

Chase Harper, A. (2020). *Time Management Hacks: How to Stop Procrastinating, Increase Productivity, and Get More Done in Less Time.* Coppell, Texas.

Cherry, K. (2020, March 26). *The Cognitive and Productive Costs of Multitasking.* Verywell Mind. https://www.verywellmind.com/multitasking-2795003.

Cherry, K. (2021, March 19). *How Maslow's Famous Hierarchy of Needs Explains Human Motivation.* Verywell Mind. https://www.verywellmind.com/what-is-maslows-hierarchy-of-needs-4136760.

Colleges and Employers Seek Well-Rounded Applicants, Not Just Busy Ones. Career Vision. (2020, October 22). https://careervision.org/colleges-employers-seek-well-rounded-applicants-just-busy-ones/.

Common Note-taking Methods. Common Note-taking Methods | University of Tennessee at Chattanooga. (n.d.). https://www.utc.edu/center-academic-support-advisement/tips-for-academic-success/note-taking.php.

Covey, S. (2021). *The 7 Habits of Highly Effective Teens: 52 Cards for Motivation and Growth Every Week of the Year.* FranklinCovey.

Davenport, B., & Morris, J. (2020, November 17). *The Ultimate List of Core Values And How To Find Yours.* Live Bold and Bloom. https://liveboldandbloom.com/05/values/list-of-values.

Determination. Urban Dictionary. (n.d.). https://www.urbandictionary.com/define.php?term=determination.

Dowd-Higgins, C. (2014, June 8). *8 Things I Learned As a Recovering Workaholic.* HuffPost. https://www.huffpost.com/entry/8-things-i-learned-as-a-recovering-workaholic_b_5101182.

Duckworth, Angela, L. (2016). *Grit: The Power of Passion and Perseverance.* Simon & Schuster.

Duncan, A. (n.d.). *Education: The "Great Equalizer".* Encyclopædia Britannica. https://www.britannica.com/topic/Education-The-Great-Equalizer-2119678.

Frankl, V. (2006). *Man's Search for Meaning.* Boston: Beacon Press

Gilkey, C. (2019). *Start Finishing: How to get from Idea to Done.* Boulder, Sounds True.

Growth Mindset. The Glossary of Education Reform. (2013, August 29). https://www.edglossary.org/growth-mindset/#:~:text=The%20concept%20of%20a%20growth,inform%20how%20they%20teach%20students.

Heyck-Merlin, M. (2016). *The Together Leader: Get Organized for your Success-and Sanity!* San Francisco: Jossey-Bass, a Wiley Brand.

Living a Life of Balance: Women of Faith Study Guide Series. (2006). Thomas Nelson.

Mayo Foundation for Medical Education and Research. (2019, May 11). *7 great reasons why exercise matters.* Mayo Clinic. https://www.mayoclinic.org/healthy-lifestyle/fitness/in-depth/exercise/art-20048389.

MediLexicon International. (n.d.). *Why is sleep important? 9 reasons for getting a good night's rest.* Medical News Today. https://www.medicalnewstoday.com/articles/325353#summary.

Muhammad, Anthony. (2015). *Overcoming the Achievement Gap Trap: Liberating Mindsets to Effect Change*. Solution Tree Press.

Oates, W. E. (1971). *Confessions of a Workaholic.* Abington, Nashville.

Petsinger, D. K. (2017, October 10). *How to Have a Successful Career and a Fulfilling Personal Life.* Lifehack. https://www.lifehack.org/632646/how-to-have-a-successful-career-and-a-fulfilling-personal-life.

Robbins, P., & Harvey, A. (2004). *The New Principal's Fieldbook: Strategies for Success.* Alexandria: Association for Supervision and Curriculum Development

Robinson, B. E. (2014). *Chained to the Desk (Third Edition): a Guidebook for Workaholics, Their Partners and Children, and the Clinicians Who Treat Them.* New York University Press.

Sasson, R. (2021, May 1). *What Is Self-Discipline - Definitions.* Success Consciousness | Positive Thinking - Personal Development. https://www.successconsciousness.com/blog/inner-strength/what-is-self-discipline/.

Sleep Disorders. Sleep Disorders | Anxiety and Depression Association of America, ADAA. (n.d.). https://adaa.org/understanding-anxiety/related-illnesses/sleep-disorders.

Sussex Publishers. (n.d.). *Procrastination.* Psychology Today. https://www.psychologytoday.com/us/basics/procrastination.

The Benefits of Getting a Full Night's Sleep. SCL Health. (n.d.). https://www.sclhealth.org/blog/2018/09/the-benefits-of-getting-a-full-night-sleep/.

The Workaholics Anonymous Book of Recovery (2005). World Services Organization

To Be a Great Leader, You Have to Learn How to Delegate Well. Harvard Business Review. (2021, April 1). https://hbr.org/2017/10/to-be-a-great-leader-you-have-to-learn-how-to-delegate-well.

Tracy, B. (2010). Goals! *How to get Everything You Want – Faster than You Ever Thought Possible.* San Francisco: Berrett-Koehler Publishers, Inc.

Tracy, B. (2017). *Master your Time Master your Life: The Breakthrough System to Get More Results, Faster, in Every Area of your Life.* New York: TeacherPedigree

Tracy, B. (2010). *The Power of Self-Discipline: No Excuses!* Boston: Da Capo Press

WebMD. (n.d.). *Stress Management: Ways to Prevent and Relieve Stress.* WebMD. https://www.webmd.com/balance/stress-management/stress-management.

Wei, P. B. J. (2021, February 23). *We Become What We Think About Most Of The Time - Earl Nightingale.* Due. https://due.com/blog/we-become-what-we-think-about-most-of-the-time-earl-nightingale/.

Why Having a Daily Routine Is Important? Check Our Examples! TimeCamp. (2021, April 26). https://www.timecamp.com/blog/2018/11/daily-routine/.

Other titles from Higher Ground Books & Media:

Raven Transcending Fear by Terri Kozlowski

The Power of Knowing by Jean Walters

Forgiven and Not Forgotten by Terra Kern

Through the Sliver of a Frosted Window by Robin Melet

Breaking the Cycle by Willie Deeanjlo White

Healing in God's Power by Yvonne Green

Chronicles of a Spiritual Journey by Stephen Shepherd

The Real Prison Diaries by Judy Frisby

The Words of My Father by Mark Nemetz

The Bottom of This by Tramaine Hannah

Add these titles to your collection today!

http://www.highergroundbooksandmedia.com

Do you have a story to tell?

Higher Ground Books & Media is an independent Christian-based publisher specializing in stories of triumph! Our purpose is to empower, inspire, and educate through the sharing of personal experiences.

Please visit our website for our submission guidelines.

http://www.highergroundbooksandmedia.com

Made in the USA
Las Vegas, NV
08 December 2021

36661072R00074